Advance Praise for

Creating Contagious Commitment

"The Tipping Point is a brilliant computer model of change initiatives as they unfold in large, complex organizations. Change agents need to be informal, keenly aware of the different needs of different types of people, and committed to their purpose. This book shows what to do and what happens along the way, both in the model and in real life."

—Art Kleiner, author,
Who Really Matters* and *The Age of Heretics

"At last! A book that gives us a concise overview of organizational change management plus a practical approach for action. How many times have we heard about projects that fail because of inadequate change management? Finally, a practical, cost-effective solution via the Tipping Point simulation. Bravo!"

—Helen Sims, Vice President, InfoSENTRY Services, Inc.

"For the first time, it is feasible for the majority of change initiatives to succeed! ... An articulated and accessible approach to exploit the Tipping Point model and uncover the levers of change in your organization."

—Tim Dempsey, President, TimDempseyConsulting

"Innovative methods used for introducing the concepts of organizational change to employees are both fun and creative. What really stands out with this book is its accessibility; its direct applications to the world of work; and its practical strategies for effectively managing organizational change."

—M. Shields, Ph.D., School of Business, Christchurch College of Education, New Zealand

"This book is a starting point for anyone involved with leading or driving a business change. Once you have a sense of the levers that are key to spreading change, you will be ready to consider your business change in a far more realistic light."

—Roger J. Bushnell, Business Performance Specialist

Creating Contagious Commitment

Applying the Tipping Point to Organizational Change

Andrea Shapiro, Ph.D.

2003, second printing, *revised*
2004, third printing, *minor revisions*

Published by
Strategy Perspective
Hillsborough, North Carolina
http://www.4-perspective.com
ccc@4-perspective.com

ISBN: 0-9741028-0-6

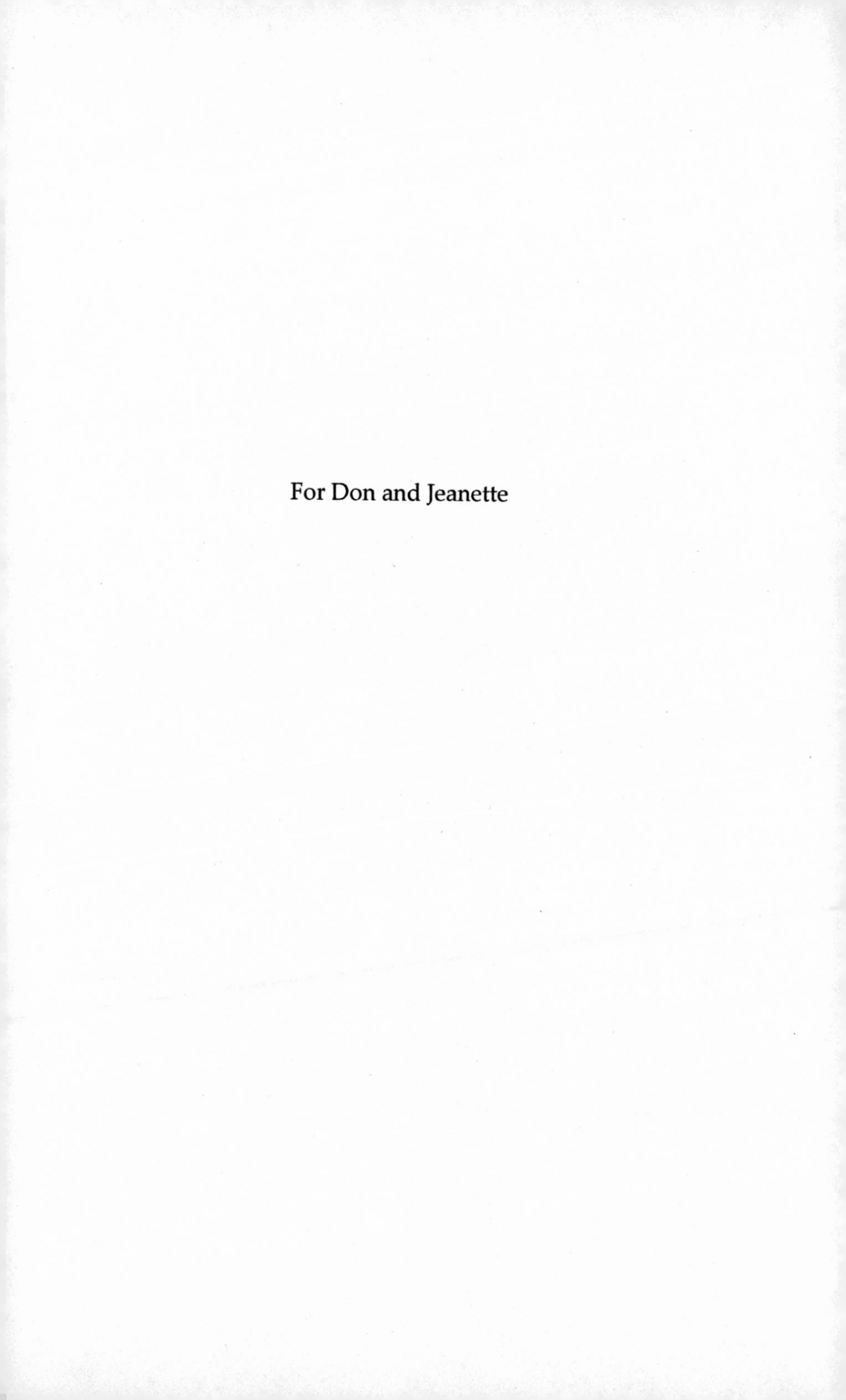

For Don and Jeanette

Contents

Introduction

An organization's ability to learn, and translate that learning into action rapidly, is the ultimate competitive advantage.
—Jack Welch

Some years ago, I asked the manager responsible for implementing ISO 9001 at a high-tech company how the change was going. At that time, they had accomplished quite a bit in manufacturing, but they were seriously bogging down in engineering. His response was, "It's going fine—except for the people." The image of a disembodied change progressing perfectly, but leaving behind employees, who were supposed to change, was amusing. Yet this is exactly what we often attempt. We work hard at the details of new processes or new technologies, but expect magic metamorphoses of the people expected to use those processes and technologies. We simply forget or ignore that organizations change when people in them change—when people become part of the change and accept new and different and better ideas about getting work done.

The foundation of any change is an idea. A change is successful when people in the organization embrace the idea behind it and spread their enthusiasm for it to others. If it doesn't spread, it's dead. This book is about the forces that give momentum to change and thus promote its spread.

Our e-everything world is pulsing with change, and the rate of change is constantly increasing. In an article in *CIO Insight*, Christopher Meyer of Ernst and Young's Center for Business Innovation illustrates multiple cases of the uncertainty, volatility, and business failure that come with this increased rate of change. A company's future success, perhaps its very survival, may depend on its ability to increase its own internal capability to take advantage of external change. If we don't adapt to external change, our competition will. Internal change is the key. Organizations must be able to effectively implement internal change to improve the way that they do business—and do so quickly.

To gain competitive advantage, leaders make a diverse array of changes to their organizations designed to improve the way they do business. Such changes include serving customers better, improving quality, making the supply chain more transparent, increasing morale, getting product to market faster, reducing risk, being more innovative, or developing and deploying tools to increase efficiency. The list of organizational changes encompasses the many ways that an organization can get better at what it does.

Yet the life cycle of many organizational changes follows a similar—and all too familiar—pattern. To fill a business need, leaders marshal forces to implement a change initiative. It could be supply chain management, customer relationship management, six-sigma quality, knowledge management, or many others. An executive and his or her team weigh the options and recognize the value proposition that the change can offer the organization—and the dangers of not implementing it. Next comes delegation. Implementation is often assigned to a vice-president of Human Resources or Information Technology or another area without line responsibility. Then a project plan is developed, including budgets, milestones, and pert charts. Money begins to flow to implement it. People are hired, incentives are laid out, and infrastructure is built or purchased. There is a major internal marketing campaign that attempts to bring everyone on board with the new initiative. Information on the change is disseminated using various media—including generic training on the change, posters, Web pages, mass emails, logo mugs, and so on.

Despite the media campaign, cynical comments about "program du jour" or "the emperor's new clothes" persist in the hallways. Other employees demonstrate their apathy by nodding in agreement at the need, the plan, and the leaders but sit firmly on their hands when it is time to take action. The project plan and the media campaign create a great deal of commotion, but they are too often followed by a big fizzle. Despite the monetary investment, despite the media campaign, despite the skill and energy of the implementers, despite the promise of competitive advantage—the company fails to realize the intended benefits from the initiative.

This story is repeated in company after company and change after change. In *Leading Change,* John Kotter estimates that 85% of companies fail to achieve needed transformations. He delineates actions leaders need to take to reduce this high failure rate. In "Why Do Employees Resist Change?" (published in the *Harvard Business Review*), Paul Strebel reports that 50–80%

of change efforts in Fortune 1000 companies fail. He argues that this stems from employees not recognizing what is driving the change and the value it can bring to the business and to themselves. In another *Harvard Business Review* article, Larry Hirschhorn calls the success rate for organizational change "abysmal" and puts the blame on managing change efforts as discrete projects rather than as monolithic efforts. In *Managing Transitions,* William Bridges attributes the problem to failure to recognize that people need time to go through psychological steps of giving up old ways before embracing new ones. I believe that all of these explanations are right, and they all provide pieces of the puzzle. But there are more pieces than just these. Even with all the pieces, we don't have the whole picture. The whole picture is more than the sum of its parts. For a change to be successful, we need a more systemic view that can put the pieces into a coherent whole.

Too often and in too many changes, I have seen the lion's share of the effort, money, and time go toward assessing the needs and selecting the change to fill them, into the technical and project management aspects of implementation, and into internal marketing. What is left over goes into supporting the people expected to make the change and into creating an environment to influence people's attitude toward the change. The poor success rate of organizational changes reflects this inattention.

The high-tech firm described in the first paragraph was never able to extend their ISO 9001 success from manufacturing into their engineering departments. They invested in ISO process templates, hired auditors, and put a massive internal marketing campaign in place. Everyone was expected to attend the same half-day course, independent of their job or how ISO was going to affect it. Graduates of the half-day course received ISO 9001 decorated mouse pads and coffee mugs—still available in local garage sales. Few engineers or their direct managers saw the value of documented processes to themselves or to the quality of the company's product; some saw it as a threat to their creativity. Although the firm did achieve ISO certification, the success was short-lived. Without understanding or appreciating ISO, people documented processes but didn't feel a need to follow them. Ultimately ISO was reduced to a dreaded annual audit ritual. This undermined the company's previous success in manufacturing, because engineering processes inevitably affect manufacturing. Even though the documented processes were in place, without the corresponding change in people's attitude the change ultimately resulted in little added value to the company. Organizations simply don't change unless the people in them change.

The core of this book is the Tipping Point model of change. It is a new dynamic and systemic model that can help us understand how organizational change really happens and how to achieve real results from it. The Tipping Point is rooted in organizational theory and real-world practice, but by integrating lessons learned from public health and systems thinking its power goes far beyond existing models of change. It helps us look inside an organization and think about what is happening to the people involved in making or impeding a change. It helps provide a theory for how ideas spread that can be leveraged to make the changes both successful and sustainable. The Tipping Point has also been implemented in a computer simulation. The simulation allows users to experience the dynamics of change, and it provides a focus for dialogue and learning to improve change implementation strategies.

The Tipping Point uses an analogy between the spread of disease and the spread of change. Public health professionals have studied the factors that make the difference between containing a disease and creating a serious epidemic. The purpose of this book is to help you turn the lessons from public health *inside out* to create an epidemic of enthusiasm for a change that is important to your organization's success. Leveraging the analogy between the spread of disease and the spread of an idea, you can create contagious, sustainable change. The Tipping Point also looks at the critical role of advocates and how they diffuse change through the organization. It defines a critical mass of advocates, demonstrates its importance, and explores how leaders sustain and support it.

Systems thinking is part of the arsenal needed to turn the lessons from public health to our advantage. It gives us the tools to step back and see the big picture, and helps overcome the fragmentation of thinking linearly and the tendency to confuse the puzzle pieces with the puzzle itself. The basic systems thinking concepts that are used in the Tipping Point emphasize the interdependence of all the actions that we can take to create change. Further, they demonstrate the futility of seeking a single silver bullet to generate transformation.

The Tipping Point model spells out combinations of actions that leaders can take to create an environment that fosters change. The model groups people according to their attitude toward a change at any given time. As people's attitude toward an organizational change evolves, they move between the attitude groups or pools. The model introduces levers of change, which are actions that leaders can take. These levers must be addressed to influence people's commitment to change. No single lever of change is a panacea; the levers' impact comes from how they interact with each other. All the levers need to be addressed or considered, with attention to the corporate culture and the nature of the change. No prescription works for every change or for every organization. The Tipping Point model provides a framework to make better decisions about using the levers. The framework provides insight that can be applied to different organizations and different changes.

The first three chapters of this book provide background on change and organizational theory, public health concepts, and systems thinking. Along with this background, the basic ideas behind the Tipping Point model of change are presented with examples that illustrate them. Chapters 4 and 5 explain the model in more detail and give illustrations of how it can be applied to change initiatives. The last chapter focuses on putting the Tipping Point to work to improve change implementation. It includes a case study in which the computer simulation is leveraged to successfully implement supply chain management in a technology organization. The case study goes into greater depth than the application examples that pepper the rest of the book. The chapter ends with a checklist to help assess your organization's readiness for a change initiative.

In my experience, some people want to thoroughly understand the motivating theory, and others want to delve immediately into the model—and learn by applying it. The book is designed to help you do both. If you want to understand the foundations, continue reading from here. If you prefer to get immediately to the Tipping Point, then jump to Chapter 4, Tipping Point: A New Model of Change. You can always go back to review the foundational chapters after you have a better understanding of the model or even after you have applied it to your own business and experienced the results.

Chapter 1

Alive with Change

Thousands of years ago, Heraclites said, "Change is the only constant." What was true in ancient Greece is magnified today. Since the time of Heraclites the drivers of change have grown and intensified. This chapter outlines drivers of change in today's business environment and some influential, though static, models of organizational change. The truth is that change changes. The static view of organizational change represented by these models, though useful, is no longer sufficient in today's business environment. To address this deficiency, the last section of this chapter introduces the Tipping Point, a new dynamic model of change for today's organizations.

Change Is about People

> It is not the strongest of the species that survive, nor the most intelligent, but the one most responsive to change.
> — Charles Darwin

Responding to the PEST

To thrive, an organization must be capable of creating value and competitive advantage from the political, economic, social, and technological (PEST) constraints that act on it. PEST forces can make opportunities appear quickly, but they can disappear just as quickly. So a business must be able to broaden its goals and improve the way it thinks about and does work—and do so rapidly. Expanding a business's goals demands organizational changes. Such changes range from the very large, such as merging two business units, to quite small, such as changing the focus of a company's online newsletter to make it a tool to increase customer satisfaction. Other examples of organizational change efforts could include moving an entire firm to a different computer network, changing the compensation structure to reflect new corporate needs, putting a customer relationship management system into operation, increasing workforce diversity, implementing computer-based training, or creating a usable knowledge management system.

It is clear that organizations must be able to respond to changes driven by the PEST to remain competitive. But competitive advantage does not come from change for its own sake but change that makes organizations more adaptable, nimbler, better able to leverage the PEST and even influence it to their own gain. They will be more responsive to customer needs; their products will have strong market positions; and they will be better able to attract the best employees. Without the ability to adapt to the PEST, companies cannot compete.

Despite the need for change, organizations experience both questioning of and inertia to important change initiatives that can become deliberate undermining. This has been true in the past and continues to be true today. Consider, for example, the serious dilution of total quality management (TQM). It went from a rigorous statistical methodology to reduce variation and increase quality in manufacturing to a management catch-all that means everything from customer orientation to people management. Similarly, proponents of business process reengineering estimate that 50–70% of such efforts fail. Enterprise resource planning programs (such as SAP, Oracle, or People Soft) have had mixed results and thus encountered resistance despite the recognized need that they fill to manage the supply chain and manage resources. It is estimated that 55% of customer relationship management programs fail, despite the importance of maintaining and sharing customer relationship data within a company.[i] To face the challenges of the PEST we need a fresh, new way to think and talk about organizational change; we need a new way to understand how change happens in organizations.

Organizational Change at its Core is about People

Organizational change is a planned effort to improve a business's capacity to get work done and thus improve its effectiveness. Organizational effectiveness includes the ability to solve problems, learn from experience, achieve goals, and take advantage of external change. It is tempting to believe that we can make the changes that are vital to our organizations by modifying organizational charts, improving processes, or adding new technologies. Although organizational change might include new technology, new processes, and new organizational charts, it is more than any of these in isolation or all of them in combination. It is fundamentally a change in people. Stated simply, organizations change when people in them change. Organizations change when people think differently about their work and approach their jobs in new and creative ways. Real change happens within organizations when employees, who are presented with a new way of working, shift their attitudes and beliefs about how work gets done.

Real change happens when people realize that the change makes them more productive or more efficient or better able to serve the customers' needs, and thus they embrace the change. The seed of real organizational change is an idea—a new idea about how work gets done. We know that ideas can be contagious. When ideas are about new and better ways of working, we want to make them spread; we want to make them "catchy." To do so, we must create an environment that helps make good ideas contagious—an environment that fosters the spread and acceptance of a needed organizational change.

Defining Organizational Change
What: A planned effort to increase capacity and improve effectiveness.
Why: Respond to or leverage PEST forces.
How: Organizations change when people in them change.

Successful change implementation involves decisions that are centered around what are often called "hard" and "soft" areas. The so-called hard areas involve such things as project planning, implementing software, and installing new computer networks. The soft side or the people side of change involves the decisions and actions designed to help employees embrace change. The effects of hard-side decisions are easily observed, measured, and adjusted. Soft-side effects tend to be subtler and more difficult to observe—making them more difficult to measure. Because it is easier to measure and assess progress with the hard side, it is not unusual for it to get more attention than the soft side. Yet attention to the people side of change is at least as important as attention to project planning or new technology.

For example, a change initiative could fail because a computer network was not installed properly. However, even if the network is installed perfectly, if employees do not use the new process or the new tool that the network supports then the change fails. Even more critical, if the problem is with a new computer network, fixing it is generally straightforward. However, it is not as straightforward to fix people's attitude that the latest change is a "flavor of the month" and will go away soon. Thus, attention to the people side is often the difference between success and failure.

The best organizational change is useless unless it is implemented and becomes part of how people do their work. Unless it is put into operation and used, the business sees no gain from it. Many things—both hard and soft—must coalesce to implement a change successfully in an organization. The Tipping Point model of change focuses on the area of greatest leverage—the people side of change. It describes how leadership can help create an environment that encourages people in the organization to adopt a change. It looks at the function of those who advocate and those who resist change, and how each can make a difference to employees feeling committed to seeing it through to success or just waiting it out.

To illustrate the people side of change, let's consider the story of an organizational change effort at a software development firm. New market demands required them to implement a quality initiative to remain competitive. Such an initiative is an example of the kinds of changes that companies make every day to grow and prosper in an environment of change. It makes clear the importance of people's attitudes to successfully implementing a change. The company and the change are presented here. In Chapter 4, Tipping Point: A New Model of Change, we will revisit this example to show how the Tipping Point sheds light on implementing this quality program.

Improving Quality at Serious Software[ii]

A medium-sized software development firm, which we will call Serious Software, operates in a very competitive environment—providing customized business software for medical professionals, such as doctors and dentists. In this environment, Serious Software made its reputation on quick turnaround rather than high quality. The software designers and testers were proud of their ability to respond to customers' unique demands by creating new software quickly. However, the world around them changed. Due to economic pressures, quality became central to their customers' expectations. To improve quality, management introduced a new step—called code inspection—into the software development process.

Code inspection is a methodology for designers to review each other's code in a formal setting. The primary goal is to improve quality immediately by reducing defects. A secondary goal is increasing all designers' familiarity with software that they did not design but with which they might have to interface in the future.

Though code inspection is clearly a process improvement change, it also involves changes to the way that people look at their work. For code inspection to succeed, designers must recognize and embrace two distinct ideas. First, they must believe that quality software is as important as responding quickly to customer demands. Second, they must be convinced that code inspection is an effective way to improve quality. Without these changes in designers' attitude and belief about their work, code inspection cannot improve quality. So this change, like most others, is fundamentally a change in ideas about how work gets done.

Employees' attitude toward the quality initiative was key to its spread at Serious Software. This is not unique. People's attitudes can impede or facilitate change—it can make the difference between success and failure. The Tipping Point addresses how change spreads, so we will revisit this company after introducing the model in more detail. It will help us understand what happened—and how Serious Software could have improved their implementation.

Models of Change

No theory—no learning.
— W. Edwards Demming

A model organizes the world that we experience. It is a way to simplify and identify the salient and most important aspects of any phenomenon. Simplification, by its nature, hides detail. A good model eliminates the clutter and brings the important aspects to the surface, helping us make sense of our experiences of the world. There are two types of models: mental models and formal models. Mental models are our internal images of how the world works. We naturally create them to make our understanding of the world coherent. Formal models are theories that can be articulated mathematically or via language or in a computer simulation.

Both mental and formal models arise in the same way and serve a similar purpose, but they have one very fundamental difference. Mental models are internal understanding. No one can see mine or question them or improve them. In fact, like most people, sometimes I'm not even aware of my own internal models that drive my understanding of the world. In contrast, formal models are public. Anyone who understands the mathematics or language that they are written in can both see and scrutinize a formal model. Thus a formal model can become an effective way to share perceptions and even develop new ideas.

Mental Models and Formal Models Help Us Make Sense of the World by Integrating Discrete Events.	
Both mental models and formal models arise in the same way. We abstract the essence from many discrete events and generalize across them. They both serve the same purpose—to create an understanding of how a system works. In particular, a model helps us understand what behavior to expect from a system and how it will respond to stimuli. Mental models are tacit and to some extent are unique to each individual. Formal models are public and can serve to create shared understanding of a phenomenon.	
Advantages and Disadvantages of Using Models	
Value Added	*Potential Pitfalls*
• Enhance understanding by bringing out the most important points. • Provide a focused starting point that includes language necessary for shared understanding.	• Oversimplification can hide important points and mask interactions. • There is potential to be ensnared by a particular simplification and fail to recognize its shortcomings.

Models, whether they are mental or formal, result from integrating individual, distinct events into a cogent whole. We abstract the essence of the discrete events and then generalize across them to create a model. Thus, models, mental or formal, are simplifications of phenomena that serve to create our images of how the world works. The important question with respect to models is *not* whether they are right or wrong. Since all models are simplifications, they are all inaccurate to some extent. The important question is whether or not they are useful—whether they help us improve and succeed.

There are two ways a formal model of change can improve results. (1) As an aid to understanding, it can provide a focused way to examine an organizational change. A good model brings out the most important and relevant points. It helps guide the questions to ask—questions that improve the likelihood of finding areas of leverage and high impact. (2) As an aid to communication, it endows us with a common language to discuss and plan the change process. With a common language, all the players responsible for implementing a change can communicate clearly about the implementation and what they expect from aspects of their implementation strategy—as well as what they expect from the change itself. By highlighting the most important points and by providing a language, a formal model helps those responsible for implementation create a common mental model of successful change.

Using Models	
Aid to understanding	*Aid to communication*
Highlight the important and relevant areas needing attention and energy.	Provide a common language that aids planning and decision making.

There is no shortage of models of organizational change. The five models that I outline briefly are those of Kurt Lewin, Marvin Weisbord, William Bridges, Daryl Conner, and John Kotter. They all make important contributions to how we understand organizational change and to the Tipping Point. You can find more detail on them in Appendix 1: More on Models of Change. The goal in this section is to look briefly at the contributions that each of them make to the Tipping Point.

Lewin, Weisbord, Bridges, Conner, and Kotter each address different aspects of implementing organizational change. Lewin introduced the idea that change is a process. It requires shaking up the old status quo and providing a framework for a new status quo. Clarifying the case for change is essential. Weisbord emphasized that we need to look at many interacting factors to understand organizations and make changes within them. He also recognized that there is both a formal and informal structure in every organization. Effective leaders must take advantage of both. Bridges recognizes that it takes time for people to go through psychological phases before they can accept a new change. Because real change takes place within people, it is essential to account for this time. Conner identifies two important roles to creating change: advocates and sponsors. Advocates recognize the value of the change, and sponsors have the authority to sanction it. Without these two key players organizations cannot change. Kotter stresses the importance of leadership and lays down eight steps for those who lead change. Leaders who follow these steps demonstrate their commitment to a change.[iii]

Five Models of Change

Lewin—Change is a process that requires unfreezing the status quo.

Weisbord—The organization is a system. We need to understand how the components interact to understand how to make change happen.

Bridges—People need time to go through psychological phases before they can accept a new change.

Conner—Two key roles in creating change are advocates and sponsors.

Kotter—Leadership has a key role in change.

All of these models have important insights on organizational change. As you read further on the Tipping Point, you can see how their ideas contributed to it. All of these models have value, but none of them focuses on what is happening in the organization to spread the idea. More is needed to better understand what people in the organization actually do to spread the change and to shed light on how a positive attitude toward a change can spread.

Remember that an organizational change is fundamentally an idea—an idea about how to improve the way that work gets done, an idea about how to be more productive, more creative, more competitive, more efficient—just plain better at what we do. A successfully implemented change is an idea whose acceptance spreads across an entire organization. No matter how good an idea is, if it is not accepted by the organization, it is not successful. If it does not result in people changing the way they work, it is not successful.

Creating a New Model of Change

A house is built by wisdom and
established by understanding.
— Proverbs 24:3

The history of the Tipping Point simulation development explains some of its strength. It was initially derived from existing theory of organizations (especially the five authors mentioned in the previous section), systems, and public health, but experience was needed to actually put numbers to the theory and create a computer simulation. To do this, I used my own experience both as a target of change and as a manager of employees expected to implement change. Further, I interviewed a small group of people who had been responsible for implementing a number of change initiatives. The group had well over seventy-five years of change management know-how among them. I used their expertise on defining the interrelationships in the simulation. After creating a working prototype of the simulation in 1997, I took it on an extensive road show to gain feedback from organizational leaders, graduate students and professors in business, and teams with experience in organizational change. With this feedback, I modified and improved the Tipping Point simulation. Since then it has been enhanced several times.

In its current form, the Tipping Point simulation has input from literally hundreds of change sponsors, change leaders, managers, and people affected by change. This input gives it a great deal of face validity. That is, the variables in the model interact in ways that are consistent with people's experience. This helps people think about change in a new way. Playing with the computer simulation in a workshop provides a focus for dialogue on change, which allows change leaders and managers to learn from each other. This makes it possible for them to create a shared vision not only of their change but also of their implementation strategy.

It would be nice to have a computer simulation that spits out the exact recipe for implementing an important change. However, all organizations and all changes are different, and there is no single recipe for change. So no single simulation can provide specific answers for every change. Nonetheless, the dynamics are similar across organizations and changes. The Tipping Point simulation offers a way to experiment with those dynamics in a safe, low-risk environment. This can help team members learn—from each other—and create a shared mental model of those dynamics. A shared mental model combines and refines the knowledge of each team member. A shared mental model helps teams create a more effective implementation plan that addresses interactions that might otherwise have fallen through the cracks. This platform for experimentation that fosters dialogue is the primary value-add of the Tipping Point workshop.

In a Tipping Point workshop, it is not unusual for people to challenge the simulation—because they place too much emphasis on the actual numbers. They seem to be portraying the Tipping Point simulation as some sort of predictive tool—as if it were saying, "If you put 5% more on this variable, then change will happen 2.5 months earlier." This misses the point completely. The numbers are representative. No two organizations are the same, and no two organizations can use the same recipe to implement a change. However, the structure of the simulation, which involves four attitudes toward a change and seven change levers and the interactions between them, is relevant to every organization. Understanding this structure and addressing all the levers of change are keys to successful change implementation.

Though questioning the Tipping Point simulation on the basis of the numbers that it generates lacks value, questioning it on the basis of the underlying structure adds value. Questioning on the conceptual level can be the first step in grasping the underlying model and gaining insight from it. As we know, not everything captured in the model applies to every organization, and conversely there are things missing for any given organization; so thorough questioning also provides a jumping-off point for adapting the concepts in the Tipping Point model to a given organizational change. Arguably, the most important value-add from questioning the underlying structure of the model is that it sparks serious discussion about change and about how ideas spread and thus helps create a shared understanding within a team.

The Tipping Point

> A great many people think they are thinking when they are merely rearranging their prejudices.
> — William James

The Tipping Point offers a fresh, new model that frames organizational change in terms of the spread of ideas. It is about a word-of-mouth epidemic—a positive epidemic of change. It draws out the importance of advocates, who are people who accept and apply a change and who demonstrate its value to others in the organization. It outlines the role that leadership plays in supporting the change by modeling desired behaviors and ensuring that rewards and infrastructure are in line with the change. It shows how, with commitment from advocates who are supported by leadership, we can make the changes that organizations need to leverage business opportunities.

Based on existing organizational theory, the Tipping Point model also draws heavily on two fields: systems thinking and public health. Systems thinking is a disciplined methodology for seeing the whole—for seeing how the parts fit together to form a whole. It is concerned with the system-wide structure that drives the events we experience. It helps us see how the behavior of a system results from the interconnection of its parts, and how its behavior evolves through time. Public health also contributes to the language needed to understand and create constructive change. Epidemiologists know the characteristics that distinguish diseases that spread quickly from those that do not. As change leaders we need to turn those characteristics inside out. We need to find the characteristics that motivate the spread of a change.

The Tipping Point model captures important dynamics of change. It helps people see potential side effects of their actions, and it sparks new ideas about implementation. It examines seven levers of change—actions that managers can take to facilitate change. These seven actions are divided into two categories: people support and environmental support. The people-support levers are actions that leaders can take or foster that directly affect employees' attitudes toward the change. The environmental-support levers are less direct but equally important. They form the underpinning that provides the support for the change. Both types of support are necessary, in varying combinations, for a successful change implementation.

The model has also been captured in a computer simulation that brings it to life. The Tipping Point computer simulation gives organizations a systemic, dynamic way to think about change. It is not a technique to follow or decision-making tool that gives the "right" answer. When used by teams to create a common mental model, it leads to better, more robust implementation strategies. The following portrayal is about a digital wireless equipment manufacturing company with $250 million in annual revenue that used the Tipping Point when implementing a customer relationship management (CRM) system.

The Tipping Point Simulation in a CRM Implementation

A fast, expanding digital wireless equipment firm with five locations distributed across North America was growing beyond its ability to give its customers the care they needed and expected. The firm had no databases for lead generation; rather, every salesperson tracked his or her own prospects. There was no way to leverage the information in the sales force's heads and use it to generate strategies for turning leads into customers and to accurately forecast sales. An even bigger problem was the lack of connection between the sales force and what was happening at the other end of the process—in customer service. The firm could not tell if particular customers were having persistent problems that needed to be addressed or if a single problem surfaced across several customers. Without a tracking mechanism, each problem appeared unique. This lack of information presented a problem for customer service and for sales, both of whom could have used the information to better serve the customer. The firm decided to address this problem with a CRM system. The new CRM system would integrate their sales and customer service, enabling them to present a consistent, informed face to their customers.

The firm implemented this CRM system at a very turbulent time. Due to market forces, it was reevaluating its product line. As a result of the reevaluation, the firm dropped two mature products that had been bread-and-butter sources of revenue in favor of newer products that had much greater potential for growth. The new products were more complex, integrating several digital wireless services (Fax, phone, paging, messaging, etc.) So the firm was developing new devices for the market, which included new networked hardware and software, while implementing a new CRM system for their internal needs.

As a high-tech firm at the leading edge of digital wireless, it is not surprising that they began the CRM implementation thinking of it as a computer network and database project. They were very focused on the so-called hard side areas—especially those focused around the CRM technology. However, the project sponsor recognized that the implementation team needed to broaden their idea of change—to realize that they were embarking on an organizational change that impacted their employees. She had to make it clear that the best CRM system was successful only to the extent that employees used it and exploited its capabilities.

The Tipping Point simulation helped give them the perspective on the CRM implementation that they needed. Representatives of customer service and sales, together with the project sponsor and the project manager, participated in a workshop that used the computer simulation. As teams vied with each other to win at the game, they began a dialogue that included the people side of implementing CRM. They developed new ideas about organizational change—ideas that they shared as a team. They realized that their plan put too much emphasis on the technology. In the days that followed the workshop, they modified their implementation plan. Through the course of the implementation they used the new language and the common mental models derived from the Tipping Point workshop to keep them on track—to help them ask the right questions when they encountered problems.

It would be wonderful to report that this firm implemented their CRM system 100% on time and within budget. Actually, they were several months late but fairly close to budget. By bringing the system online and in use—with both sales and customer service data in one place and in use to improve their customer relations—this firm has joined an elite group. Their CRM system is part of the 15% to 50% of organizational change implementations that end in success.

By reading this book, I want to help you join this elite group—to make your organizational changes both contagious and sustainable. The book provides a framework that is general enough to be applied to many changes and many organizations and specific enough for real action planning. You will find both theory and application examples throughout the book, so that when you are done you will be ready to apply the Tipping Point model of change to your organization.

A Focus for Dialogue Enhances Learning

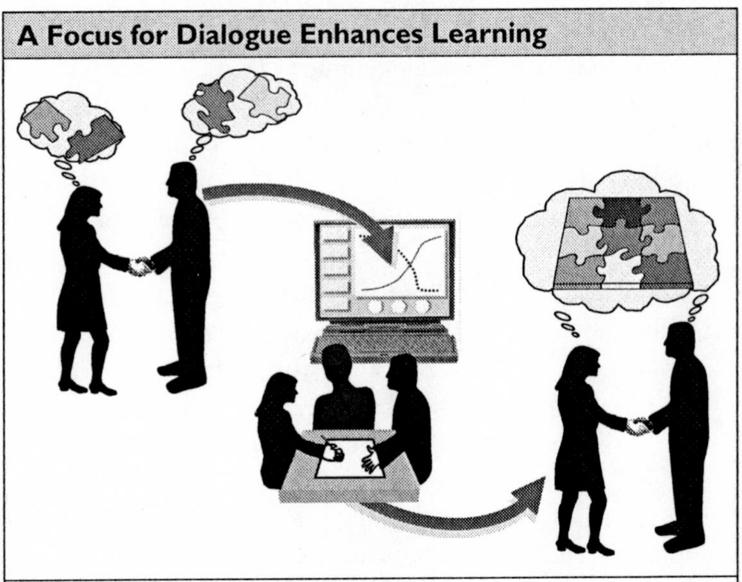

The Tipping Point computer simulation is *not* an answer machine. Rather it provides a focus for dialogue and discussion in a low-risk environment. Team members, using the simulation together, talk about change and experience the interactions inherent in change as they try out change strategies in an atmosphere of friendly competition.

In workshops using the Tipping Point computer simulation, team members often spontaneously stand up to cheer as their strategy unfolds in the simulation. Participants discuss trade-offs and costs as the simulation runs. They have been known to vigorously debate their strategies. Through this atmosphere of friendly competition, team members learn from each other and gain a common shared view of change implementation.

Moving Forward

Key Concepts

- Change is constantly driven by the ever-changing political, economic, social, and technological (PEST) milieu in which we do business. Organizational change is needed to adapt to, take advantage of, and even influence the ever-changing PEST.

- Most organizational change initiatives fail. We need a new view of organizational change. The Tipping Point combines theory from systems thinking and public health with the best of change management and organizational theory to provide a new way to think of change.

- A model is an organizing theory that helps us make sense of the world. There are many models of change. The Tipping Point is an innovative model that creates a new language and a way to create a common mental model of change implementation.

Points to Ponder

- Do you understand the external factors that are driving your change, the advantages of making the change, and the threats of remaining with the status quo? Does everyone in your organization? Do people agree on the drivers?

- Can you articulate your personal mental models, beliefs, and assumptions—which drive your actions and decisions—on how change happens in organizations? Do others affected by your change initiative share them?

- When you initiate a change are you considering the people who actually have to change the way that they do their work? Are you leveraging their expertise?

Chapter 2

Lessons from Public Health

Epidemiologists have studied the spread of infectious disease for many years. They have a handle on the conditions, situations, and behaviors that cause a disease to spread. Our job is to take the lessons they have learned and turn them inside out. We need to create positive epidemics—epidemics of enthusiasm and commitment for an organizational change. We need to find the characteristics that motivate change, so acceptance becomes contagious—and spreads throughout the organization. Luckily the analogy between the spread of a disease and the spread of an organizational change is quite direct. The Tipping Point model leverages what epidemiologists have learned to help leaders create effective, sustainable change in their organizations.

Spreading Good Ideas

> Those who cannot change their
> minds cannot change anything.
> — George Bernard Shaw

To illustrate how lessons learned from public health apply to implementing changes within an organization, think about how the flu spreads. The key to flu spreading is contact; it spreads when people who are contagious with the flu come in contact with well people. What happens? Some of the well people begin incubating the disease. After a period of time, some of the incubating people go on to become contagious and are thus able to spread it to others. Some incubators—depending on many interacting factors, such as the status of their immune system, the virulence of the flu strain, how much sleep they get, and other factors—never get sick. They just return to the pool of well people.

Contact Is the Key to the Flu Spreading

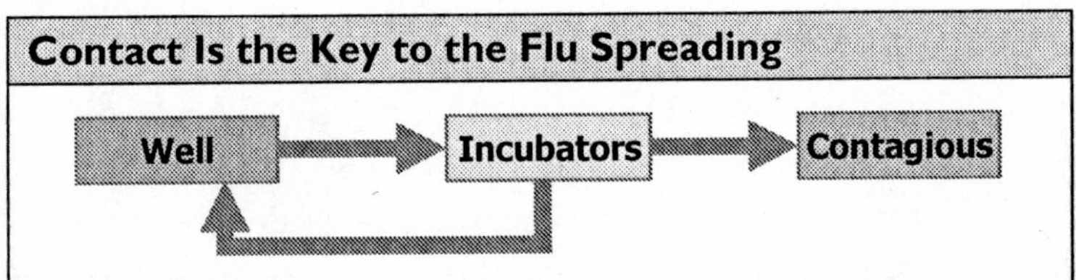

We can think of people as falling into one of three categories with respect to the flu; they are well, incubating, or contagious. The flu spreads when contagious people come in contact with well people. Some of the well people begin to incubate the flu. Depending on their immunity, the virulence of the strain, and other factors, some of the incubators will go on and become contagious themselves, further able to spread the flu. Others will never express symptoms and just return to the well pool.[iv]

We can apply the familiar pattern from the flu to organizational change. In the organizational change analogy we are talking about the spread of ideas—ideas about new and better ways of working. We're talking about a positive epidemic. Ideas spread when people with expertise, experience, and enthusiasm *advocate* them. These advocates of an organizational change are "infected" with a new way of doing work. When people have this enthusiasm, they talk to others. They talk to people who have never heard of the idea or who feel disconnected from it, people who are *apathetic* to it.

When advocates talk to apathetic people, one of two things can happen. Some of the apathetics begin to think about it; they mentally test it against their own beliefs and experience. We say that they begin to incubate the idea. Other apathetics will just ignore it. They may nod in agreement, but they take no action and remain apathetic. Among those who are incubating, some may, with time and experience, become advocates themselves. Other incubators will fail to see the value and become apathetic again. Some advocates will remain advocates further able to spread their enthusiasm for the idea. Others will decide that the organization is not really serious about the change and return to the apathetic pool (or even leave the company).

Organizational Analogy

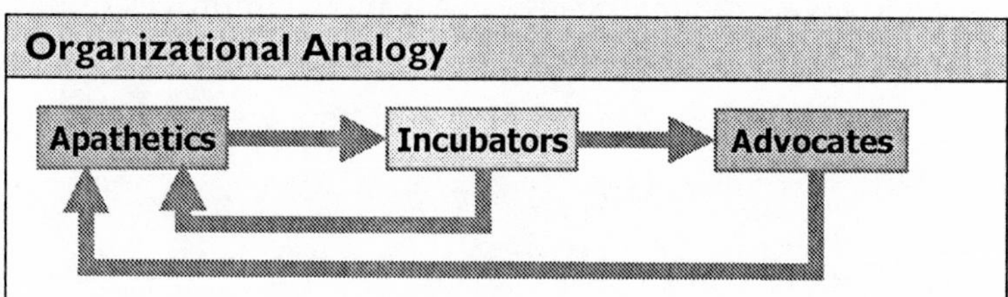

We can think of people as falling into one of three categories with respect to the their attitude toward an organizational change. They may feel completely disconnected from it or unaffected by it, in which case we call them apathetic. They may be thinking about how it affects them or how it will work in their environment, in which case we say that they are incubators. They may be completely infected with enthusiasm for it, in which case we say they are advocates. (Later you'll see a fourth category, resisters.)

The attitude of enthusiasm toward the change spreads when advocates come in contact with apathetics. Some apathetics will begin to incubate the new idea. Some incubators will go on to become advocates themselves; others will be unconvinced and return to the apathetic pool. Ideally, we want people to remain advocates, but if the change is not supported by the organization, advocates can also slip back to the apathetic pool.

In the right environment the enthusiasm of people infected with an idea can become contagious. Applying the model of a contagion and associated concepts from public health to social questions is not new. Ryan and Gross used this concept to study Iowa farmers' acceptance of new seed corn in the 1940s. In 1978, Thomas Schelling applied the contagion model to numerous social situations; some of these areas include people crossing a busy street in groups large enough to feel safe, attendance at seminars, and the so-called white flight to the suburbs. John Sterman recently examined the dynamics of a word-of-mouth epidemic to new product marketing. Applying the contagion model to organizational change in a way that improves results is an important advance offered by the Tipping Point model. It helps us see how change happens and how we can foster its spread.

Interacting Factors

One important lesson from public health is that you cannot consider a disease separate from the environment in which it is happening or the people that it affects. The environment, the people with the disease, and the disease all interact to affect how it spreads. First consider an example that illustrates how important the people with the disease are to how it spreads. European diseases, such as measles and smallpox, were serious but by the era of New World exploration, they were not real plagues in Europe. However, these same diseases wiped out entire Native American villages. These Native Americans did not have the immunity that Europeans had developed over generations of living with those diseases. Today, cholera provides an example of the effect of the environment on how a disease spreads. Cholera spreads quickly in areas without clean water supplies, but it is virtually unknown where water is clean.

The spread of ideas works analogously—there are numerous interacting factors that affect how fast an idea propagates. A good idea could spread like wildfire in one environment but have no effect in another. The analogy to the spread of change within an organization is quite direct, if not perfect.

Analogy Between Spread of an Organizational Change and Spread of the Flu

There is a close—almost one-to-one—analogy between the factors that affect the spread of an idea such as a change initiative and those that affect the spread of a disease. Understanding this analogy gives us the opportunity to apply the lessons learned from public health to make changes in our organizations contagious.

Factors that affect the spread of the flu		*Factors that affect the spread of change*
The virulence of the flu strain	↔	The intrinsic value of the organizational change
Contacts between contagious and well people	↔	Contacts between advocates and apathetics
Environmental factors, such as level of sanitation and medical care	↔	Environmental factors, such as bonuses for successful implementation

The speed with which an idea or an organizational change spreads depends on the innate value of the idea and the amount of contact between the advocates of it and people who are apathetic to it. The rate of spread is also affected by environmental factors like rewards and recognition, leaders who lead by example, and infrastructure investments that support the change.

In his book *The Tipping Point*, Malcolm Gladwell examines how social changes spread by word of mouth. He examines the three factors that make the difference between changes that spread rapidly and become social epidemics and those that are stagnant and eventually die out. To describe these three factors, he coined the following terms: *content*, *carriers*, and *context*. In the case of the flu, these correspond to the flu strain itself, the people with the flu, and the environment where the flu is (or is not) spreading, respectively. Although Gladwell does not specifically consider organizational changes, they are nonetheless examples of social changes; they involve the spread of an idea through the interaction of people, the environment, and the idea itself. Under the right conditions they have the potential to grow into epidemics. Looking at content, carriers, and context from an organizational change perspective can shed light on how a change initiative can spread.

Content is analogous to the virulence of a disease. In organizational change, it refers to the actual value of the idea, which Gladwell describes as its "stickiness." Intrinsic value helps an idea become sticky and thus spread. The stickiness of an organizational change is the value that it brings to the business. It is the idea's innate ability to improve the way work gets done—to improve the company's ability to serve customer needs. The more an organizational change is designed to leverage the political, economic, social, and technological factors influencing the company and make it more productive, the stickier it will be.

Carriers are those who are infected with the idea; they are the advocates described previously. Gladwell points out that not all carriers are equal, which he calls the Law of the Few (described in more detail shortly). Having a few key people in an organization who have the respect of many others will help an idea spread more quickly. This is similar to the Pareto principle or 80/20 rule. (Two often cited examples are 80% of the work is often done by 20% of employees, or 80% of revenue is from 20% of customers.) Leverage comes from finding the 20% of the population that has the respect of and the connections to the other 80%—in other words, finding the 20% with the potential to spark an epidemic of change.

Nothing happens in a vacuum; *context* is the environment where the change is happening. In the case of diseases like flu, context is the public health system, the sanitation, and so forth. In the case of an organizational change, it is the support—or sometimes lack of it—that management provides for the change. The importance of support should never be underestimated. Few, if any, changes succeed without infrastructure, incentives, and leaders who demonstrate commitment.

Content, carriers, and context interact in ways that can make huge differences in the spread of commitment toward a change. For example, a very good organizational change in a non-supportive context will not spread, and the firm will reap no reward from it. On the other hand, a very good change, with the right advocates, can take off after small improvements to the context that make it more supportive of the change.

Content, Carriers, and Context Interact to Determine How Quickly an Idea Will Spread

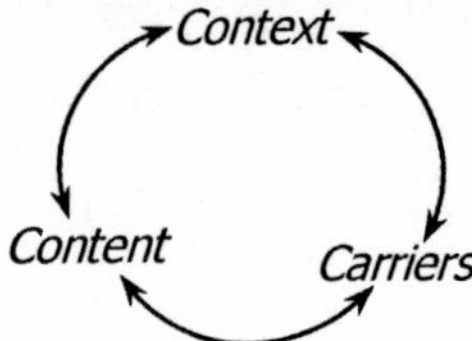

In his book *The Tipping Point,* Malcolm Gladwell describes three main interacting factors—*content, carriers,* and *context*—that determine the course of an epidemic. These factors can also be applied to an organizational change. *Content* is the strength of the change. *Context* is the environment in which the change initiative is happening. *Carriers* are the characteristics and behaviors of those infected with enthusiasm for the change.

A standing ovation is a very simple example to help illustrate the interaction of content, carriers, and context. Think back to the last concert or play you attended. Perhaps it ended with a standing ovation for the performers. A standing ovation usually begins when a few people set an example by standing up to applaud the performance. Whether the standing ovation spreads or not depends on the quality of the performance, on where the performance is held, and on who begins the ovation and what they do. First consider carriers. Enthusiastic applause from front-row audience members that everyone can see is more likely to spread than similar clapping from people standing up in the rear. Just as important is the content. A standing ovation spreads differently than quiet, polite applause and still differently from booing or throwing tomatoes. Clearly content and carriers interact; reserved enthusiasts from the back will spread polite, sitting applause more easily than a standing ovation. Context is just as important. The auditorium itself, whether it is a huge outdoor arena or a small community playhouse, interacts with the content and carriers to determine whether or not the standing ovation spreads to the entire audience.

It is worth noting that no one designs or controls a standing ovation. It spreads itself through the interaction of content, carriers, and context. The real power in implementing organizational change is to create the environment that fosters the content, carriers, and context to spread the change in much the same, natural way as a standing ovation. In *A Simpler Way*, Margaret Wheatley and Myron Kellner-Rogers advise leaders to adjust the way that they think about their responsibilities. They say that a leader's role is to create connections, provide information, make resources available, and let the organizing processes work.

The organizing processes work through interaction between content, context, and carriers. Any change initiative will spread differently in different organizations. That is, the same content yields different results with different context and carriers. This is similar to a disease. It spreads rapidly through a population that has not built up immunity and does not have access to adequate medical care, and it can be stopped quickly in a population that has built up immunity or better medical care. Similarly, a change initiative might be easily adopted and lead to great cost savings or increased productivity in one organization and fail to be implemented or yield the desired results in another. You could say that the environment tailors the change—no change is exactly the same in two different environments.

I once heard Russell Ackoff, a leader in applying systems thinking to business challenges, tell a story about a CEO who failed to recognize the importance of context and carriers to implementing change. In a meeting with all his general managers, the CEO compared the efficiency of all the processes that were common to all the facilities. He noticed that relative to the others, no single plant was more efficient in all the processes. For example, suppose shipping in one plant was more efficient than all other plants, whereas in another plant billing was better than all of its sister plants.

This CEO decided that for each common process he would pick the most efficient one, from whichever plant it originated, and implement it across all the plants. The CEO was warned that he was taking a very non-systemic view of the processes. His plan did not consider the effect of the environment on a process. It did not consider that all the points of interaction between a process and the rest of the plant contribute to its efficiency—or inefficiency. It did not consider the specialized skills of those people doing (or interacting with) each process in each plant.

Nevertheless, he went ahead with the plan. Millions of dollars and a great deal of effort later, the result was that all the processes in all the plants were less efficient than before. The CEO didn't take context or carriers into account. He could not see that a process was efficient in one plant in part because of its interactions with other processes in the plant, in part because of the people who executed it and even in part because of the environment around the plant. He failed to recognize that content, carriers, and context all interact to make a process efficient.

Ackoff's example does not imply that no practice can ever be reused in a different environment. Rather, it implies that successful reuse demands first knowing why the practice works, how its environment influences it, and how it influences its environment. Only after all these factors are understood can reuse bring value.

Resistance

There is another useful analogy from public health to help us understand organizational change—resistance. We know that people can develop resistance to a disease, sometimes even complete immunity to it. Resistance is all too common in organizational change. People who are incubating a change sometimes begin to push against it. They may fail to see the value or believe that it is inappropriate to the organization or feel it threatens their own position. So they begin to resist the change. This gives us a fourth pool of people in the organization—resisters. The four pools of apathetic, incubator, resister, and advocate form the attitude pools considered by the Tipping Point.

Resistance: A Fourth Attitude Toward a Change

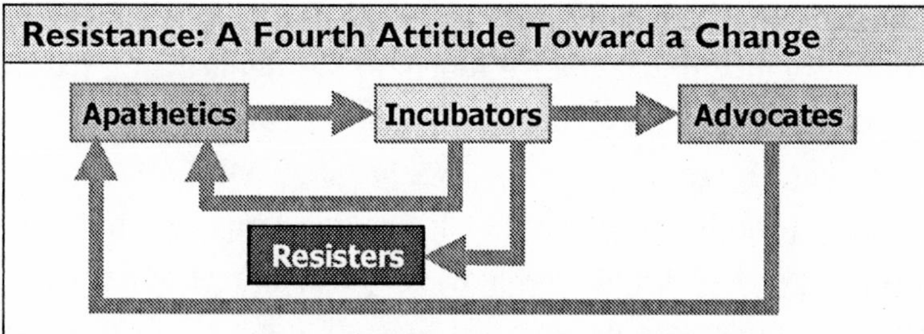

Some people will resist an organizational change. To lead change effectively, it is important to recognize that resistance is inevitable, and some resistance can be useful. Resistance can stem from constructive concerns about the change to cynicism to fear. To address resistance competently, we must know its source.

Resistance to change can come in several forms. The first is legitimate, constructive concerns about a change, of which there may be many. The change could be incomplete or too much of a cultural jump for the organization or not understood; perhaps it may even be inappropriate or ill-timed. Resistance that stems from constructive concern should be thought of as an early warning system. A great deal can be learned to strengthen a change—or even avoid failure—from resisters with genuine concerns. Such resistance can spark exploration for better methods of implementation or improvement to the change itself. When constructive concerns are aired and acted on suitably, they become a source of innovation and enhance the likelihood of success. However, if the corporate culture interprets legitimate concern as a challenge to the change or to management's authority then, in the best case, an opportunity to learn and improve is lost. Worse, it will probably cause the resister to become more covert in his or her resistance—thus having more potential to undermine successful change.

A marketing director at a large telecommunications company told me that she sees it as her *responsibility* to question every organizational change touching her department. Occasionally, this tactic backfires on her, and she is labeled a troublemaker. However, her experience has shown that when she is consistent and constructive with her questions, the result is usually positive. Often problems with the change initiative or its implementation are revealed through honest, constructive questioning. Addressing these problems saves the company time and money, often with a positive effect on her own department and budget, and it yields a stronger change initiative.

Unfortunately not all resistance is constructive. A more dangerous source of resistance is from too much exposure to changes that were supposed to be important improvements but ended up as nothing more than slogans on coffee mugs. Resistance resulting from overexposure to change initiatives that were not fully implemented, despite their potential, can be very damaging. When employees have seen changes over hyped in the past they begin to associate needed changes with meaningless hype. Even worse, changes are sometimes misrepresented, such as by claiming benefits for employees that in fact are nonexistent. Either case creates an atmosphere of cynicism about change. The potential to create cynicism underscores the importance of only undertaking organizational changes that are important, presenting them honestly, and being prepared to fully sponsor them through to successful implementation.

A third form of resistance comes from fear. It could be fear that the change will result in people losing jobs, authority, influence, or bonuses. These outcomes make people feel that the future is outside of their control. It is the stuff of rumors and unrest. The reality is that depending on the change, these things are a possibility; some may lose their influence or even their jobs. Candor and honesty is the only way to approach this source of resistance. If a merger or reengineering effort will result in a lay-off, spell out the reasons and the numbers as clearly as you know them. If you do not, you can be sure that the rumor mill will portray them as many times worse. Good information is one way to slow the flow of rumor. Knowing the real picture and believing in its accuracy gives people a sense of control and has the potential to alleviate some resistance.

Sources of Resistance

- Concern with the change or its applicability
- Exposure to hyped and unsupported changes in the past
- Fear of loss

From these three sources of resistance, it is easy to see the role of trust. Targets of change need to trust that it is safe to air their concerns. They need to trust that a change that they put effort into is real and not just hype. They need to trust that they have been told both the upside and the downside of a change. Trustworthiness of the sponsor and leaders of the change is vital. Trustworthiness may not eliminate resistance, but untrustworthiness will definitely increase it.

Besides coming from different sources, resistance can manifest itself overtly or covertly. Overt resistance can be a source of valuable information, if it is presented constructively and listened to. Covert resistance sabotages a change. In *Managing at the Speed of Change,* Daryl Conner recommends developing a culture that questions change openly. He even suggests developing a course on how to resist change, where people learn how to present their concerns constructively. The flip side is that there must be safety from reprisals for raising concerns, and people must feel that management will consider the issues that they raise and act on them appropriately.

Make the Case for Change Clear—and Do So Honestly

A large call center that operated under contract to another firm embarked on a new quality initiative. The targets of the quality initiative were the customer service representatives (CSRs) who answered the calls. The call center wanted to ensure quality, as measured by metrics defined by the contracting firm. The quality initiative was presented to the CSR team as a training initiative with the goal of raising the call quality by raising the ability of every CSR.

All the supervisors received literature that they were to share with their people. This literature indicated that there would be increased call monitoring to find areas where training could improve overall customer service and thus improve the quality metrics. This literature further explained very specifically that the call center leadership was *not* trying to weed out bad apples. However, their real intention was to improve quality by finding those employees who were responsible for any problems and reprimanding or replacing them.

It did not take long for the CSRs to realize that they were being lied to, as they were written up for minor quality problems that had been ignored previously. Employees became jaded about the company's true commitment to improve quality through focused training. They did not feel safe enough to raise their concerns to management, but they raised them at the water cooler. When the training did not materialize, many began covert resistance by just doing the absolute minimum of customer service. Morale dropped seriously, affecting even the most competent CSRs, with a corresponding drop in quality. The call center lost two of its best CSRs and experienced its first serious threat to contract renewal in ten years.

The lesson from the call center is that this change failed because it was not approached honestly. Improving quality is a good change, so the content is valid. The carriers were ready; they wanted to improve quality. Had they been told the nature of the change honestly, it was more likely to succeed. Instead the context created by the call center operator was toxic, and they lost the very employees that they wanted to retain. Worse yet, it soured the remaining employees—the necessary carriers—for future change.

The story of the call center is not uncommon—most organizational change initiatives fail. Between 50% and 85% of change efforts are either abandoned before implementation or are implemented and fail to live up to their financial potential.[v] Failing to live up to potential is often a result of ignoring context and carriers. The following account is adapted from the experience of a company that we will call Medical Machines.

Knowledge Management at Medical Machines

Medical Machines had been very successful in automated hospital bench-top diagnostic tools. Their innovative medical test devices had significantly increased the diagnostic capability of smaller hospitals, offering their customers both cost savings and an increase in the types of patients that these hospitals could serve. As a result, Medical Machines enjoyed significant market share.

A new start-up company entered the market with smaller, more portable, and more automated equipment, initially designed for home nursing care and for physicians' offices. These devices used wireless transmission to increase their devices' capabilities by connecting to major hospitals when necessary. The start-up got Medical Machines' attention when they began marketing their devices to small hospitals, thereby winning over some of Medical Machines' customers.

To compete, Medical Machines developed newer, smaller, wireless-capable devices, thereby venturing into areas in which they had little experience. The sales force lacked familiarity with the new products, and there was poor communication between sales and engineering. As a result, Medical Machines began having problems meeting promises made to customers. They felt that a knowledge management (KM) system would help engineers and sales support personnel communicate on new projects and existing engineering change orders. This would allow them to leverage the learnings about each product and from each sale and thus avoid making promises that they could not keep.

Although a KM system requires networks and software, it is fundamentally a cultural change. Employees must view the value of their own knowledge differently. To succeed, there must be rewards for employees to share knowledge. If both engineers and salespeople do not see the value to themselves and to Medical Machines of sharing information, then even a technically perfect KM system will fail.

Medical Machines assigned the implementation task to the vice-president of information technology. From a technical viewpoint, he was the person best able to implement a KM system. His team immediately began the process of adapting a commercially available system. There was no research into understanding what aspects of the corporate culture limited knowledge sharing. Furthermore, no members of his team were targets of the change, so they lacked an appreciation of how it would be used.

Within one year, the system was made available to both engineering and sales, complete with logo mugs and a huge fanfare on the value expected. However, nothing was done to foster knowledge sharing. There had been rewards for implementing the KM software, but no rewards or recognition for sharing knowledge. Few employees saw value to sharing knowledge to themselves or to the firm. In fact, many resisted the change because they felt that sharing knowledge might be giving away their edge to bonuses and promotion within the corporation. There were also no metrics in place to measure the value to Medical Machines as a whole of sharing knowledge, so the business case could not be made for the KM system. It became a little-used and expensive piece of software.

At Medical Machines, the targets of the change—the people who were expected to use the KM system—did not understand its value. Far from enthusiasm for a new tool that could make them more productive, they felt threatened by it and thus resisted using it. People must see the value and feel supported to take the risk to do things differently.

Thinking in terms of content, carriers, and context, we can see what Medical Machines could have done better. To begin with, they mistook the content of the change for the change itself. They saw it as a technology implementation. They did not recognize the cultural changes that were needed to make it successful. With regard to carriers, they did not identify the advocates of knowledge sharing, so they were hardly in a position to support them in any way. Furthermore, no one took the time and effort to listen to the resisters' concerns, which could easily be addressed by making the business case clear and by initiating incentives for sharing knowledge. In short, Medical Machines did not create the context for change. They did not create the environment where the carriers, those employees who had knowledge to share, felt safe sharing it and making the KM system successful.

Supporting Advocates for Change

Things do not change; we change.
— Henry David Thoreau

When people *do* recognize the value of an organizational change to their own productivity and work environment, their attitude toward it often becomes positive. They get excited about it and alter their way of working. With experience they become advocates of the change. If the environment is conducive and the advocates are respected for their contribution, then their enthusiasm becomes infectious. Advocates can spread the word about the effectiveness of an initiative and how it improves their achievements on their jobs. As advocates spread the word, others may begin to consider the value of the change to their own job effectiveness. When they change the way that they think about their jobs and become committed to it, real change can spread through the organization. To return to our earlier metaphor, this is much like the way an epidemic spreads through a population.

The Tipping Point represents an organic model of change. It recognizes that change is a process and that the targets of change have a key role in its success. In *The Human Side of the Enterprise*, Douglas McGregor puts forth Theory Y to describe the behavior of individuals at work. He argues that when employees are committed to objectives, they seek responsibility and demonstrate imagination and creativity. The way to gain commitment is to be sure that people understand the purpose of an action. When they do, they exert self-direction, often coming up with better methods and doing better work. The Tipping Point builds on Theory Y. It recognizes that people who are targets of a change are typically the best people to explain a change and its value to another target of the change—especially when they know that the change is well supported by management.

The path that any change initiative follows is rarely (if ever) smooth and straight. In *New Rules for the New Economy*, Kevin Kelly describes this very succinctly by saying, "Don't confuse a clear view for a short distance." Change initiatives often expose hidden problems or create flux or make the situation worse before it gets better.

Having a clear vision of the end state is important, but it hardly means that the road to it is clear or straight. This underlines the importance of advocates. Advocates affected by the change are much closer to the action than are the sponsors of the change. They are in the best position to navigate the small dips, bumps, and plateaus between now and the end state, and to explain to others affected by the change specifically what to expect along the way.

The Path to Change is Rarely Straight or Smooth

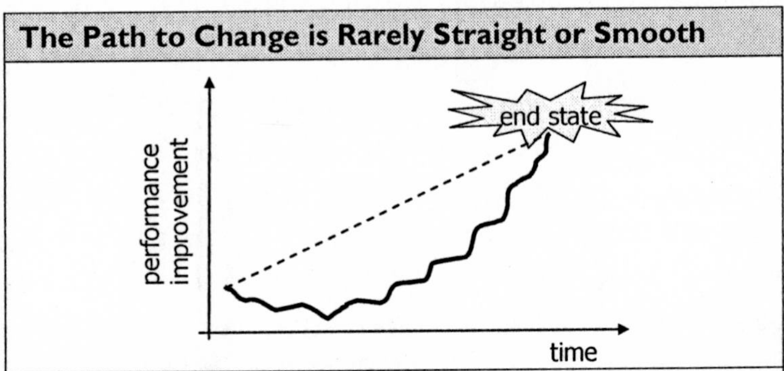

Having a clearly articulated vision of the end state is an important step in any change process. However, it does mean that the path to the vision is straight and clear. A change can be disruptive. Current methods may be good enough for the present, making the change appear like an overlay or unnecessary work. Other sources of disruption occur if the change exposes hidden problems or requires extra effort at the beginning. All of these can cause the organization's performance to get worse before it gets better—even for a successful change.

There are inevitable bumps, plateaus, and false peaks in the path to the new performance expected from the change. Advocates who are respected by their peers can help navigate the bumpy road to success.

Applying the Tipping Point model empowers the targets of the change. Rather than focusing on resistance, the Tipping Point recognizes and uses the leverage of existing advocates. A change spreads when people with expertise, experience, and enthusiasm advocate it and infect others, but there is still a role for leadership. No matter how important a new change may be—no matter how enthusiastic its advocates may be initially—the idea will *not* spread throughout the organization without support. Leadership has a key role in creating the necessary support for an organizational change. No one can get inside the heads of people who need to think differently about their work. However, leadership can create the context that allows change to happen by ensuring support for the advocates of a change.

There are two types of support that leaders can provide: *people* and *environmental* support. People support includes such things as explaining what to expect from the change, listening to concerns, and fostering contacts between advocates and others. Environmental support helps create the atmosphere for change. It includes making the business case clear to all stakeholders, putting necessary infrastructure in place, and rewarding those who support the change. If neither type of support is in place, all but the most die-hard advocates will recognize the futility of supporting a doomed change and move their energies elsewhere. If either the people or the environmental support is insufficient, there will be problems, even if the other support system is adequate. If the people support is high but the environmental support is low, then people will see the change as only happy talk with no supporting resources, creating cynicism toward it. If environmental support is high but people support is low, confusion will reign, leaving people unfamiliar with the change and confused about their roles.

Clearly leaders must attend to both people and environmental support. Ignoring either one leaves the implementation open to confusion or cynicism or both. There is no fixed recipe for success; every change is different, and every organization is unique. To create the context conducive to change, leaders must understand and apply the environmental and people support needed for their change and for their organization.

Environmental and People Support Interact

Environmental Support	Low People support	High People support
High	Confusion slows acceptance Wasted $$	With support, advocates for change help ensure success
Low	Without support for advocates there is almost guaranteed failure	Cynicism slows acceptance Wasted $$

Both people and environmental support must be adequate to foster change. If people support is high but environmental support is low, then people's expectations will be raised, but they will lack the tools to really make the change. This creates cynicism that tarnishes both the current change and future changes. If environmental support is high but people support is low, then tools will be available, but people will not know what to expect from them or how to use them.

Traditional linear thinking leads us to believe that large efforts lead to large effects. But like epidemics, the spread of ideas is not linear. Experience with implementing change initiatives demonstrates that large efforts at organizational change can have frustratingly small effects. For example, huge one-size-fits-all training programs can have little—or even negative—impact despite the investment in energy and resources. On the other hand, small efforts, like initiating informal networks to support advocates, can have significant effect. As none of us have unlimited budgets for change, time and money invested in ascertaining the most effective people and environmental support for our organization is well spent.

Another dangerous way to waste investment is by trying to create an environment of forced compliance. The "do it or else" threat is not an endorsement of a change. It does little to engender the kind of commitment that spreads under its own enthusiasm. Donella Meadows, a pioneer in systems thinking, said that systems, with all their feedback and interactions, are inherently not controllable. I would add that neither are the people in the systems; at most they can be controlled temporarily. Success comes from finding the behaviors that you want and fostering them and encouraging them to develop further.

Recognizing the Limitations of Forced Compliance

I was introducing the concepts behind the Tipping Point to a large and respected government agency. I had barely begun when someone put voice to a notion that the more politically astute people may have been thinking. She said, "We don't really need advocates. We just need compliance." For a second, I considered reminding the group that they were starting their second try at implementing this particular change. Instead, I reminded them that compliance has never spread like wildfire. True commitment never stems from fear, nor can it be forced. Contagious commitment to an organizational change develops when people understand its value to their own jobs, and they feel supported to make the change.

The group went on to use the Tipping Point computer simulation. It helped them experience how commitment can spread when people demonstrate and advocate the change to others in the organization. After working with the simulation, the group from this agency recognized the leverage that comes from supporting advocates and encouraging them to spread their commitment to others. The woman who thought that they could get by with just compliance was probably the most fervent about the lessons from the Tipping Point model. Months later, the group was still using the Tipping Point language to help assess their progress with the change implementation.

A change that is supported—by infrastructure, rewards, and actions of the leadership—and advocated by experienced and credible people is much more likely to succeed. When a change is supported, people are much more likely to listen to the advocates of change and take their experience seriously. The most powerful way to implement change is by creating the context that allows the people in the organization to grow rapidly into the change. It is leadership's responsibility to create the climate for commitment, the context that helps people understand the organizational change, provides the tools to make the change work, and creates incentives and an atmosphere in which enthusiasm and success can grow. Advocates are key to spreading good ideas. If they are properly supported, advocates help ensure success. People support and environmental support must be balanced to sustain advocates of a change to create a change that can be implemented in a timely manner and sustained.

The drivers of change are not static and an organization can be faced with implementing several changes in a short time. Maintaining people and environmental support for one change helps create the mechanisms that can be applied again and again. Eventually this can lead to a change management capability—that is, to an organization with the nimbleness to respond quickly to implement change initiatives that are needed to succeed.

Critical Mass

Enthusiasm moves the world.
—J. Balfour

Nuclear physicists developed the concept of critical mass to describe the behavior of interacting atoms and their particles. "Critical mass" refers to the minimum amount of nuclear fissionable material that is necessary to sustain a chain reaction. With less than a critical mass, there is no chain reaction (or it is not sustained) and the energy dissipates. With a critical mass, the chain reaction begins at the atomic level, gains incredible energy, and literally explodes beyond control. Physicists can create chain reactions because they have a theory that explains how to create a critical mass. A look back at theories of diffusion of ideas helps explain how to create a critical mass of advocates that under the right conditions can cause a chain reaction that leads to an explosion of enthusiasm for a change.

In the early 1960s Everett Rogers extended the study of farmers' acceptance of new types of hybrid seeds to a more general theory of how any innovation diffuses through a population. In *Diffusion of Innovation*, he described people in terms of their innovativeness or how willingly and rapidly they accept an innovation. He claimed that innovativeness is normally distributed; it has the familiar bell-shaped frequency distribution. Furthermore, he classified people into five categories according to their willingness to accept innovation. From the most willing to the least, the groups were called innovators, early adopters, early majority, late majority, and laggards.

A thumbnail sketch of each of the categories defined by Rogers helps us understand their role in advancing new ideas. Innovators, who make up about 2.5% of the population, are the venturesome types who want to try something *because* it is new. The next category on the scale of innovativeness is early adopters, about 13.5% of the population. They tend to be more judicious than innovators but are still motivated by new ideas and the possibilities they offer. The early majority make up the next 34% of the population. They are not interested in innovation for innovation's sake, but they don't want to be the last to adopt an innovation if they believe it has practical value. The late majority are the 34% who adopt an innovation just after half the population has adopted it. They wait to see that it really works and is beginning to become the standard. Finally, the laggards are the 16% of the population who are the last to adopt an innovation, if they adopt it at all. Laggards sometimes have the function of maintaining institutional memory and keeping the overly experimental types from jumping too quickly to a change.

According to Rogers, adoption of innovation spreads from the innovators toward the laggards. The innovation is beginning to become a new standard as the early majority adopt it, which paves the way for the late majority. The early majority plays the very important role of connecting the innovators and early adopters with the other half of the population, who are much lower in their innovativeness.

Innovativeness Is Normally Distributed

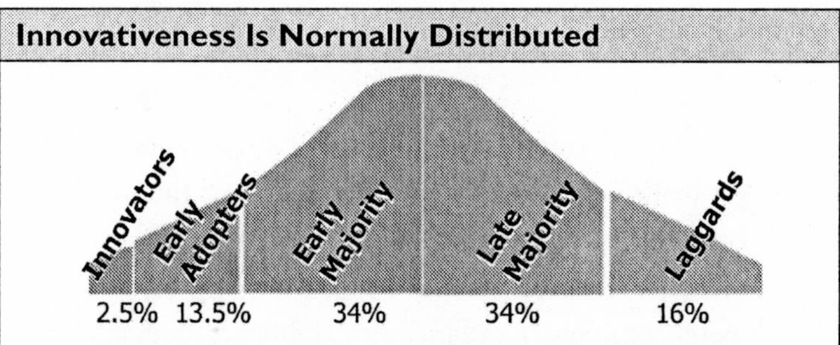

Rogers found that people's willingness to accept innovation was normally distributed, forming a familiar bell curve. Innovators and early adopters are more willing to adopt innovation. The majority is divided into the early majority, which accepts innovation more easily, and the late majority, who wait until the innovation is almost a new standard before they adopt it. The laggards are the last to embrace a novel approach or technology.

In *Crossing the Chasm*, Geoffrey Moore adds an interesting and important twist to Rogers's theory. According to Moore, the early adopters have a very different attitude toward innovations, especially new technical innovations, when compared with the early majority. Their respective attitudes are so different that the early majority does not value early adopters' recommendations. The early adopters seek the major innovations that can lead to competitive advantage, whereas the early majority look for practical, incremental solutions with clear applicability. To make matters worse, the early majority places a great deal of value on recommendations. This creates a catch-22. The early majority will not consider a new innovation without a reference on its value, but they do not value the same things that early adopters do. So the recommendations that the early majority hear from the early adopters do not influence them or their decisions to adopt an innovation. Thus, Moore refers to the transition between the early adopters and the early majority as the *chasm*. It is a huge rift that takes planning and positioning to cross.

Chris Musselwhite moves the idea of an adoption life cycle into organizational change. He describes three different change styles: originators, pragmatists, and conservers. These change styles influence people's attitude toward change in general and how they react to a given organizational change. Understanding and appreciating each style can help change leaders plan their implementation strategy.

Originators in Musselwhite's scheme correspond roughly to the innovators and early adopters (combined into one group). They are motivated by change that is radical and challenges the status quo and the existing structure. They focus on ideas, look for the new and different, and seek what is possible.

Pragmatists correspond roughly to the early majority. Finding a practical solution that works to solve a problem motivates them. They first seek change that does not affect the existing structure but will consider more radical change if it is necessary to create the advantage needed. They focus on results, look for solutions that reflect the current demands, and seek what is functional.

Conservers correspond roughly to the late majority and the laggards. If they have to make a change they prefer an incremental change that preserves the existing structure. They focus on gradual change, look to putting existing resources to better use, and seek to preserve the existing structure.

Three Change Styles		
Originators	**Pragmatists**	**Conservers**
• Future-oriented insights that can drive change • Catalysts for change • May overlook relevant details or the impact on the existing structure	• Encourage cooperation to find solutions • Adapt past experience to solve current problems • May be too willing to compromise	• Work well within existing structure • Consistent and reliable with strong follow-through ability • May delay action and discourage innovation

From Musselwhite's descriptions of the three groups we can conclude that the chasm seen in diffusion of innovation appears again in adopting organizational change. The visionary language of the originator does not speak to results-oriented pragmatists. The broad possibilities that inspire the originator feel nebulous to the pragmatist, who wants to solve the problem at hand in the most direct practical way. One challenge of successful implementation is to value each constituency group for what it brings to the table. Originators are able to see the possibilities of a new organizational change. However, they may overlook the disruption that the change can trigger. Pragmatists want to see problems solved in practical ways. They look for the no-nonsense applications of the change and how it addresses the problems. Conservers value the status quo. If they see the need for a change, they prefer it to be incremental and not disruptive to the existing structures. They also prefer that it be to an established or well-tested process that is starting to become a new standard. To be successful, change leaders must address the concerns and styles of all three constituencies.

Implementation Chasm

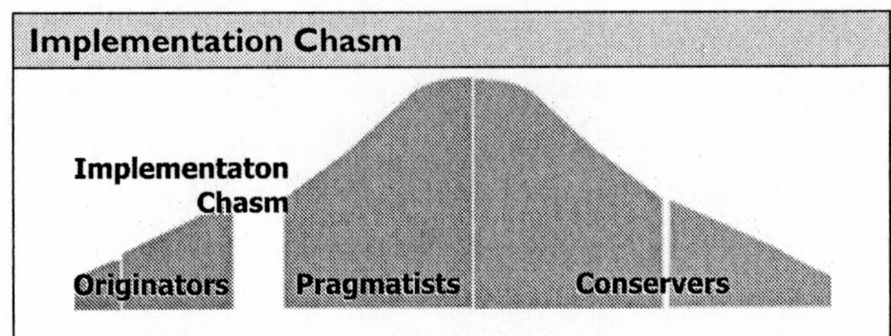

The implementation chasm occurs because originators and pragmatists tend to value different things in an organizational change. Originators are motivated by radical changes that have the potential to create a huge effect, regardless of its impact on the existing structure. Pragmatists look for changes that solve specific problems and minimize the effect on existing structure.

The concept of critical mass can clearly be imported to the language of organizational change, but we see from the works of Rogers, Moore, and Musselwhite that it becomes more complex. In physics, critical mass refers to enough material. In an organization change, critical mass is more than just enough people. A change needs to cross the implementation chasm; it requires a mix of originators and pragmatists. To be successful, it must inspire the visionary originators, but the pragmatists must also recognize its value. Pragmatists tend to seek workable, practical results. To become an advocate of a change, pragmatists need to see results and believe them to be repeatable and workable.

This creates the implementation challenge. The early advocates of a change are typically originators. They see the possibilities. They appreciate the new value add but perhaps ignore the harm to the existing structure—structure that may be serving the company well in many ways. They paint the possibilities in broad terms, but these terms do not speak to the pragmatists. Pragmatists seek functionality. Crossing the chasm between the originators and the pragmatists is the challenge. Once the chasm has been crossed, the organizational change is well on its way to becoming a standard, and it is much easier for conservers to adopt.

In his book *Leading Change*, John Kotter outlines eight steps for change leaders. Creating early wins is one of his steps. A significant change can take quite a bit of time to put into operation. An early win, such as a successful pilot program, can create credibility for the change while full implementation is in progress. Creating early wins is important and making sure that they are measured and recognized is equally significant. Early wins, which are explicitly measured, well rewarded, and broadly recognized, help pragmatists see the value. Once a change does speak to a broad cross-section of originators and pragmatists, it will have gained a critical mass. It will have enough people—and, more important, the right people—to cross the implementation chasm. Early wins bring more wins and more pragmatists. A mix of innovators and pragmatists can influence the conservers and tip the change toward success.

Advocate Skills

> It does not require a majority to prevail, but rather an irate, tireless minority keen to set brush fires in people's minds.
> — Samuel Adams

Good ideas do not spread by themselves. Ideas spread when people advocate them. The best advocates are people in the area affected by the change, who have experience with it, and who are respected by their peers for what they contribute to the product or service that the company produces. Experience with the change is key. It allows advocates to explain the value of the change in very concrete terms. It allows them to "tell stories" about the change that people can identify with.

No matter how much experience and enthusiasm an advocate has for a change, no matter how much he or she is respected for expertise, it takes specific skills to help spread good ideas. It is important to grow the pool of advocates, and it is equally important to develop skills within the advocates to spread change. Advocates must know how to listen to the concerns addressed by resisters, and to raise important concerns to leaders who can address them. They need to be cognizant of whom to get on board and of people's change style. Thus, three key capabilities for advocates of change are: skilled conversation, fluency with the law of the few, and sensitivity to people's change style.

Skilled Conversation

In some situations, skilled conversation can be almost as important as expertise with the change for spreading commitment. In *The Fifth Discipline Fieldbook,* Richard Ross and Charlotte Roberts describe the value of balancing inquiry and advocacy.[vi] *Advocacy* is convincingly, forcefully, and clearly expressing a position, and *inquiry* is seeking to understand another's position better. Advocacy requires making your own assumptions clear, distinguishing between data and opinion, and articulating the logic and reasoning behind your conclusions. Critical thinking skills are important for effective advocacy. In contrast, inquiry refers to the ability to hold conversations that openly share ideas and help expose each person's assumptions. Listening skills are prerequisite for effective inquiry. People skilled in inquiry can really hear what others say, and they seek to understand the data and reasoning behind the conclusions. They are less subject to imposing their own interpretation on others. Balancing inquiry and advocacy is a key skill for an effective advocate of a change initiative. None of us, not even the most enthusiastic advocate, has the complete and full picture. Combining multiple perspectives helps create a fuller picture. This demands inquiry skills to really hear and understand others' views and advocacy skills to clearly state your own.

Balancing advocacy and inquiry is especially important when dealing with resistance. Overt resisters often have legitimate concerns about the change or about management's true commitment to it. It is almost an oxymoron to say that concerns cannot be addressed unless they are fully understood. Inquiry is needed to understand those concerns and the assumptions behind them. On the other hand, advocacy is needed to clearly make the case for the change to someone who is apathetic or even resisting. An apathetic person is more likely to begin to incubate an idea if it is clearly stated, and all the assumptions (even the most tacit) and reasoning behind the conclusions are fully transparent.

Fluency with the Law of the Few

In his book *The Tipping Point,* Malcolm Gladwell examines factors affecting social change. He describes the law of the few, which is based on identifying three different types of people, called mavens, connectors, and salesmen, who can make the difference between a change spreading or not. *Mavens* are the people who always seem to know the important answers. They are the gurus to whom others consistently turn for advice and recommendations. *Connectors* are people who just seem to know everyone. They connect people from different groups who would otherwise not be connected. *Salesmen* have the ability to persuade, and they are driven to persuade when they really believe in something. According to Gladwell, a very few people who have these skills can make a huge difference in how—or if—an idea spreads. He calls this the law of the few because, relative to others, it does not take many of the mavens, connectors, and salesmen to make a big difference in spreading an idea.

Organizational change is one example of the types of social changes in which mavens, connectors, and salesmen can make the difference between a change spreading or fizzling out. It is important to get them on board. They are the people the early advocates need to contact. Getting them into the advocate pool and getting them in early will help spread an organizational change. Conversely, it is deadly to the change initiative if these people are among the resisters. Fluency with the law of the few is twofold. First, it requires understanding the importance of the mavens, connectors, and salesmen to spreading change. Second, it involves identifying who the mavens, connectors, and salesmen are within the organization and getting them into the advocate pool

Sensitivity to Change Style

The third skill is sensitivity to change style. Advocates need to be aware of their own and other people's change styles, whether they are originators, pragmatists, or conservers. Chris Musselwhite and Robyn Ingram have developed the Change Style Indicator, an assessment tool to determine people's change style. Advocates and other change leaders can use it to assess their own style and understand how change styles affect how people view an organizational change initiative.

It is not unusual for the early advocates to be originators. If they are to conquer apathy, they must meet each person where he or she is. To cross the implementation chasm, originators need to understand the values of the pragmatists. They need to use language and examples that will speak to them. Otherwise contacts between advocates and apathetics are not likely to result in the apathetics actually incubating the new idea. Using language and examples that speak to pragmatists will not be helpful when trying to explain the value of a change to a conserver. Advocates must understand the style of the apathetics they are contacting and what language and examples will speak to them.

Advocate Skills
Skilled conversation—balancing advocacy and inquiry in contacts.
Fluency with the law of the few—identifying and contacting the mavens, connectors, and salesmen.
Sensitivity to change styles—leverage change style when making contacts.

There is no substitute for expertise, experience, and enthusiasm when advocating a change. Good advocates are also the targets of the change; they are the managers and employees who are expected to do work in a new way. Good advocates are respected by their peers for the work they do. Good advocates are even more effective if they are also skilled at knowing how to spread the word. To this end, there are three important capabilities for advocates. Skilled conversation—balancing advocacy and inquiry—helps them listen to others and address their concerns. Understanding the law of the few helps them know whom to contact and encourage to join the advocate pool. Sensitivity to change styles helps them tune their language to the style of the person. These skills are vital to creating the critical mass necessary to cross the implementation chasm and tip the organization toward organizational change.

Moving Forward

Key Concepts

- Ideas can be contagious. When ideas are about new and better ways of working, we want to make them contagious. Lessons from public health can show us how to make an organizational change both contagious and sustainable.

- People's attitudes toward a particular organizational change will fall into one of four categories: advocate, incubator, apathetic, or resister. Advocates have experience in the change and believe that it will make a difference. Incubators are thinking about the change and weighing it against their experience. Apathetics may not know about the change, or they feel disconnected from it. Resisters are actively challenging the change.

- The three key advocate skills that help spread change are (1) skilled conversation, (2) fluency with the law of the few, and (3) sensitivity to change styles.

Points to Ponder

- Is the change properly supported? Do the sponsors of the change really believe that it will make a difference? Can they clearly explain the business case behind the change? Do they do so early and often?

- Do you know who the advocates of this change are? Is there a plan in place to support them?

- Do you know where there is resistance to this change and what it stems from? Have you talked with resisters?
- Has the change begun to cross the chasm between originators and pragmatists?

Chapter 3

Thinking Systemically

Standing on the beach to watch the sunset, we see a flat ocean. It appears to go on for a long way and then just drop off suddenly. Despite any globe that we have seen or any transoceanic trip that we have ever taken, the impression of flatness is inescapable. In *The Fifth Discipline*, Peter Senge says, "Reality is made of circles, but we see straight lines." Seeing straight lines causes fragmentation in how we perceive the world. It limits what we see—while at the same time giving us the impression that we are seeing it all. Just as looking at the horizon is only seeing part of the Earth, so linear thinking captures only part of the picture. Systems thinking is a discipline that gives us the tools to overcome this limitation. The Tipping Point relies heavily on systems thinking, so this chapter presents some of its basic concepts.

Links and Loops

> The whole is more than the sum of its parts.
> — Aristotle in *Metaphysica*

To understand what it means to think systemically, we begin with a definition of a system. Simply stated, a system is a collection of components that interact together to function as a whole. Any organization is a social system, and an organizational change is a change to this system. Organizations are embedded in larger systems—community, national, economic, industrial, and global systems. The way of the systems thinker is to think in wholes rather than parts, attend to the role of time, and understand feedback.

Systems Thinking Skills

The bright red cardinal at my bird feeder is a lovely creature and is also a system. He is a collection of components, wings, feathers, eyes, ears, and internal organs that all interact together to form a showy red bird. The cardinal has characteristics such as the ability to see, fly, and chirp that emerge from the interaction of these components. Further, the individual components of the cardinal need to be part of the whole bird to express their essential function. His wings cannot fly unless they are part of the cardinal nor can his eyes see. The cardinal—like any system—is defined not by its components but by their interactions and interrelationships. Thus, identifying components is important, but thinking in terms of their interactions is essential to systems thinking.

The interactions between components in a system result in dynamics—or system behavior. Dynamics unfold over time. Sometimes components interact very quickly, causing the resulting system behavior to appear almost instantaneously. Sometimes there are delays. One way or the other, time is always a consideration in understanding the behavior of a system. So another systems thinking skill is to look for patterns of behavior over time. These patterns of behavior—or dynamics—of the system are a result of how its components interact. The set of interacting components is called the structure of the system. In sum, the dynamics are what we experience, and they result from the interactions of the elements in the underlying structure.

Thinking in Wholes	
• A system is a collection of components that interact together to form a whole.	• A cardinal is a collection of components—all necessary to the cardinal's existence.
• Each component must be part of the whole to do its essential function.	• Each component—wings, organs, etc.—has its function only as a part of the whole cardinal.
• The whole gets its characteristics from the interactions of the components.	• The cardinal gets its characteristics from the wings, organs, and other components interacting.

Systems thinking is a disciplined way to think in terms of wholes and understand the behavior of the whole system in terms of the interactions of the components that make up it up. Three skills are key to systems thinking

- Thinking in wholes, rather than parts
- Recognizing the importance of time
- Understanding the effects of reinforcing and balancing loops

Feedback Loops

The interactions in systems inevitably lead to closed loops called feedback loops. There are two types of feedback loops—reinforcing and balancing. These form the basic building blocks of systems thinking. Each type of loop has it own characteristic dynamics that combine with other loops to create more complex patterns. Reinforcing loops always result in steady growth or decline. Balancing loops result in system behavior that approaches an asymptote or goal—either smoothly or with some oscillation.

The following paragraphs go into further detail about reinforcing and balancing loops. A couple of examples demonstrate these two types of closed loops and their application to understanding real-world problems. If you are totally unfamiliar with the notation used in closed loops, you might want to read Appendix 2: Notation of Links and Loops. This notation helps us look at the system behavior caused by reinforcing and balancing loops, and how they facilitate thinking systemically.

Reinforcing Loops

The screech that we have all heard when the speaker and microphone in a public address system get too close is a familiar example of a simple reinforcing loop. It happens when the microphone is placed where it can pickup the speaker's output. The microphone feeds this sound to the amplifier, which amplifies what it gets from the microphone and puts it back out to the speaker. Then the microphone picks up the amplified sound for further amplification. This cycle of amplification continues very rapidly until the speakers' ability to put out sound is saturated, and everyone's ears hurt.

A more business-related example of a reinforcing loop is the interaction between an employee's performance and the support that he or she gets from management. An employee whose performance goes up tends to get more support, in the form of better assignments, bonuses, needed training, and so on. This drives performance up even further. However, reinforcing loops can result in both growth and decline. An employee whose performance goes down tend to get less support, which causes performance to decline further. I don't mean to imply that management support is the only influence on employee performance. It is just one straightforward influence used for illustration, which is captured in a simple reinforcing loop shown in the following diagram.

A Simple Reinforcing Loop Example

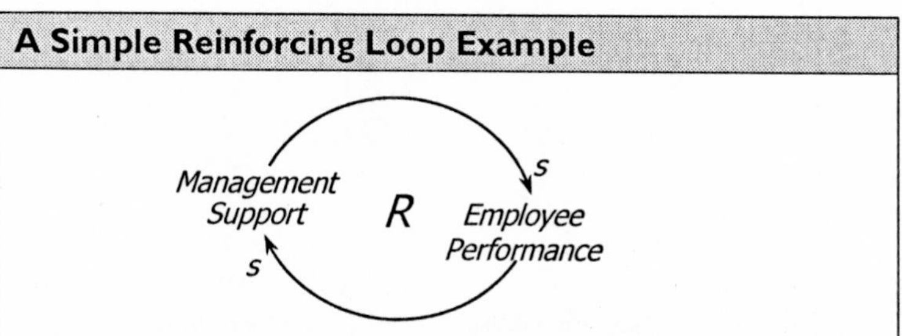

This is a reinforcing loop because *Employee Performance* drives *Management Support*, which further drives *Employee Performance*. If *Employee Performance* goes up, then (all other things being equal) *Management Support* goes up. Similarly the loop can work in reverse—to compound decline. If *Employee Performance* goes down, it will tend to drive the *Management Support* down, which further drives *Employee Performance* down.

The link between *Employee Performance* and *Management Support* is labeled with an "s" (for "same") to indicate that they move in the same direction. That is, when one goes up then the other one goes up; conversely, when one goes down the other one goes down. The loop is labeled with an "R" to depict its self-reinforcing nature.

Reinforcing loops always generate the same dynamics, which is sometimes referred to as behavior over time (BOT). They compound, or reinforce, the existing change. If the change begins as growth, then the loop will compound it to more growth. Similarly, a reinforcing loop will compound decline. If there is some decline, then the loop will compound it, leading to further decline. So reinforcing loops always yield either continual growth or continual decline.

Reinforcing Loops Yield Growth or Decline BOT

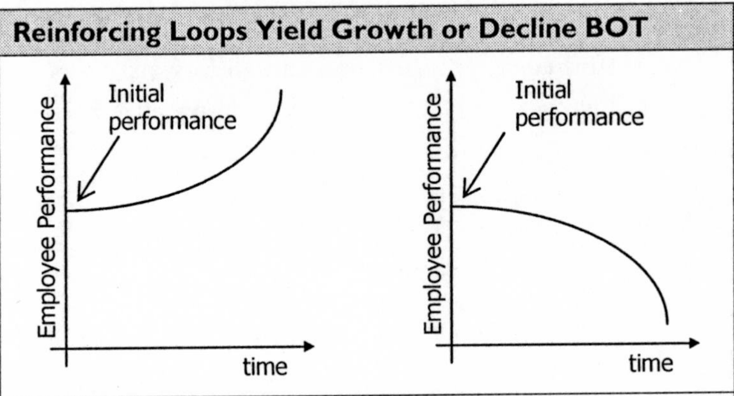

These two plots reflect the two possible behavior over time (BOT) patterns that one could expect from the reinforcing loop shown in the previous diagram (on page 71). In that reinforcing loop we saw that, Management Support can drive Employee Performance up, which drives more Management Support and so on, yielding the BOT pattern on the left.

It could go the other way. If the initial change in Employee Performance is down. The loop drives Management Support down, which would further drive Employee Performance down yielding the BOT plot on the right.

Reinforcing loops are never stable or goal-seeking. They never reach equilibrium. It is safe to say a reinforcing loop never exists *alone* in nature—because nothing can grow or decline forever. They are always mixed with some limiting factor (perhaps another reinforcing loop competing for the same resources). The effect of a reinforcing loop with whatever it is combined, is to create growth or decline. The growth or decline that is created by a reinforcing loop is called exponential growth (or exponential decline). There is more on exponential growth in the next section, titled The Power of Two. Either way, growth or decline, the pattern takes the form of the graph above. It starts off slowly and only gains momentum over time.

Balancing Loops

The other building block of systems thinking is a balancing loop. The way the heating system in your home works is a good example of a balancing loop. Working in combination, the thermostat and the furnace try to keep the temperature in the house close to the goal temperature that you set on the thermostat. When the house temperature drops below the goal temperature, the thermostat senses the difference and turns on the furnace. The furnace will remain on until the thermostat senses that the house temperature has risen above the goal, at which time it shuts off. Assuming it is colder outside, the house will begin to cool down. When the temperature drops below the thermostat setting, then the process starts all over again.

Balancing loops that have very small or no delays in them will approach their goal (e.g., the thermostat setting) very smoothly. However, for most balancing loops, delays are inevitable. It takes time for the furnace to heat the house. It takes time for the thermostat to respond to the change in house temperature. The result is oscillation around the thermostat setting, sometimes the house temperature is a bit above the thermostat setting and sometimes it is a bit below. The longer the delay, the greater the oscillation. The quicker the thermostat senses the house temperature and the faster the furnace heats the house, the smaller the oscillations in temperature.

Returning to the employee performance example, a balancing loop is also involved. The interaction between the employee's performance, the number of assignments that he or she gets, and the quality of the resulting work forms a balancing loop. As performance goes up, the number of assignments will tend to go up. We all like to give assignments to people who tend to do them well. To a certain point the employee can handle the larger workload, but after too many assignments, quality will tend to go down. Quality is a big part of overall employee performance, so the worker's performance begins to fall. With lower performance he or she will tend to get fewer assignments. With fewer assignments the employee can spend more time on each one, so quality goes back up. This drives performance up and so on. This loop will tend to oscillate around an optimum number of assignments with a corresponding performance level.

A Simple Balancing Loop Example

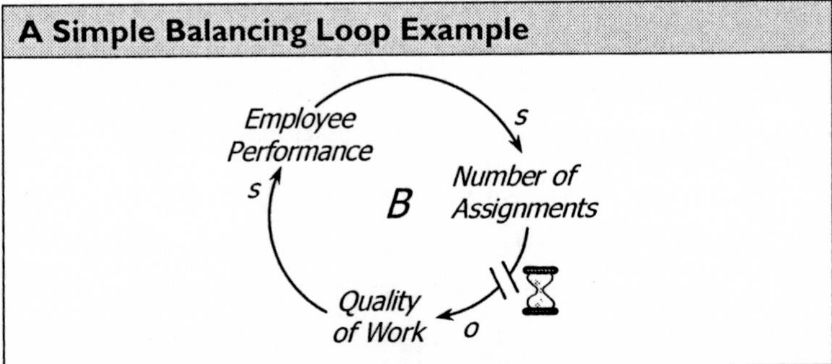

This is a balancing loop because its dynamics will balance *Employee Performance* around an equilibrium. That is, this loop will tend to drive *Employee Performance* to a stable level.

Start with the link between the *Number of Assignments* and *Employee Performance*. The higher the *Employee Performance*, the more assignments the employee is likely to get. Eventually the number of assignments takes its toll. After a delay (marked with an hourglass), the employee's *Quality of Work* tends to go down. When *Quality of Work* goes down, the *Employee Performance* goes down—because quality is an aspect of overall performance.

The link between the *Employee Performance* and *Number of Assignments* is labeled with an "s" (for "same"), because they move in the same direction. The link between *Number of Assignments* and *Quality of Work* is labeled with an "o" (for "opposite"). They move in the opposite direction; when the *Number of Assignments* goes up the *Quality of Work* tends to go down and vice versa.

The link between the *Quality of Work* and *Employee Performance* is labeled with an "s" because they move in the same direction. The loop is labeled with a "B" for balancing.

Balancing loops give very different dynamics than do reinforcing loops. Instead of steady growth or decline, balancing loops will approach a goal or asymptote. Balancing loops that have very small or no delays in them will approach the goal very smoothly. However, for most balancing loops, there are delays. It takes time for the quality of the employee's work to go down. The result is oscillation around an equilibrium performance as shown in the diagram below. Systems with more or longer delays will tend to have greater oscillation, and those with fewer or shorter delays will have less oscillation.

Asymptotic BOT from a Balancing Loop

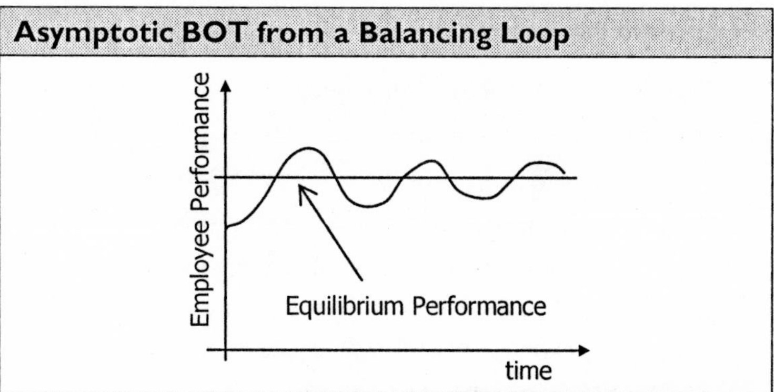

This graph of *Employee Performance* is stereotypical of a balancing loop with delays. It begins at an initial performance, which could be above or below the equilibrium. For illustration purposes, assume it is below. The performance will tend to overshoot the equilibrium because of the delays in the system. That is, it takes time for the increased number of assignments to affect performance. As performance declines, it will undershoot the equilibrium because it takes time to build up quality. The overall behavior is to oscillate around the equilibrium.

A system with more or longer delays would tend to have

greater oscillation, and one with fewer or shorter delays will have lower oscillation.

Combining Reinforcing and Balancing Loops

The two building blocks of systems thinking—reinforcing and balancing loops—can be combined to describe any system. The behavior over time (BOT) of any system is a result of the interactions of its components and the feedback loops that they form. The reinforcing loops always contribute to continuous growth or decline, and the balancing loops always contribute to goal-seeking behavior. The events that we experience are a result of the components interacting to form reinforcing and balancing loops, which display their inherent dynamics. We can easily see this by combining the balancing and reinforcing loop already described as having an effect on employee performance.

The following illustration captures both effects on employee performance. It includes the reinforcing loop that tends to drive performance up—or down—and the balancing loop that tends to drive it toward equilibrium. In this case, first the reinforcing loop would dominate and we would see steady increase (or possibly decrease) in performance, but nothing can grow or decline forever. Eventually, the effects of the balancing loop would begin to dominate, causing oscillation around an equilibrium.

Performance Is Driven by a Combination of Both a Balancing and Reinforcing Loop

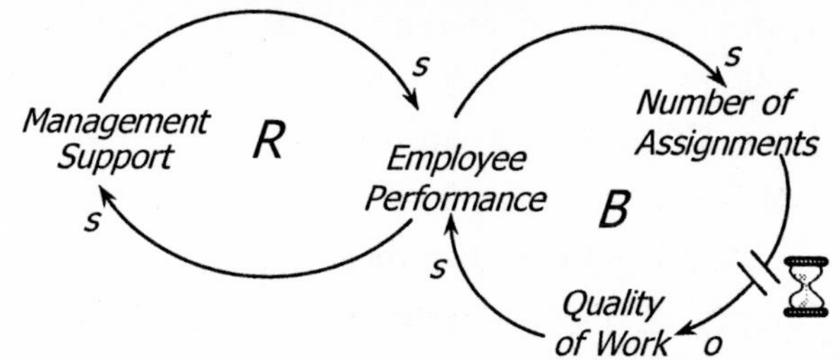

Reinforcing and balancing loops combine to describe more complex behavior. In this example *Management Support* tends to drive up *Employee Performance*. In turn, *Employee Performance* raises both *Management Support* and *Number of Assignments*. However, as *Number of Assignments* goes up *Quality of Work* tends to go down, driving *Employee Performance* down.

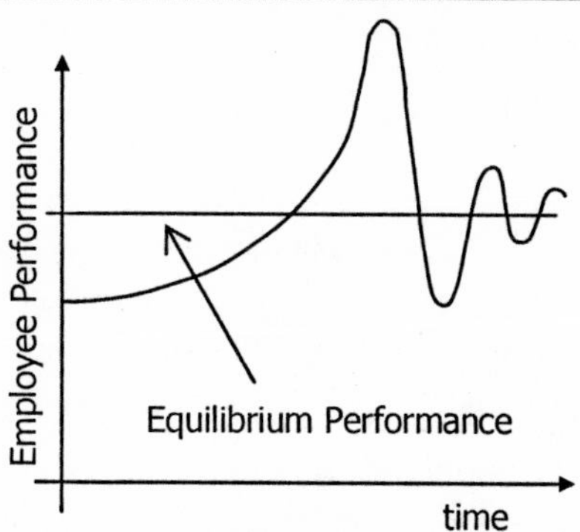

The reinforcing loop on the left of the diagram above would tend to dominate until the number of assignments got so great that it affected the employee's *Quality of Work*. Then the balancing loop would begin to dominate—driving *Employee Performance* toward its equilibrium. Due to the delay, it would tend to go below the equilibrium at first. Eventually the behavior of the system oscillates around the equilibrium.

These simple link-and-loop diagrams illustrate the potential of thinking in terms of the interaction of the components that make up a whole system. By illustrating the interactions and by identifying where the delays in the system are, we get a fuller picture of what is happening. Thinking systemically and understanding the structure that drives organizational change is critical to success. Link-and-loop diagrams are to a change leader what an x-ray is to a physician. If we become skilled at creating and reading them, then they can give us insight about what is happening inside. If organizational change were easy, then the success rate would be greater than 15–50%. Our organizations are complex systems. Skill at understanding the aspects that drive change and how they interact is key to successfully implementing change. Link-and-loop diagrams assist in making these interactions more transparent.

The Power of Two

I think there is a world market for maybe five computers.
— Thomas Watson, Chairman, IBM, 1949

It is easy to underestimate the exponential growth caused by a reinforcing loop. It is easy to be trapped in linear thinking—thinking that small efforts have small effects and that large efforts have large effects. For example, it is easy to fall into thinking linearly about change: One person today, one more tomorrow, a third the next, and so on linearly through the organization. Thinking of an idea as being contagious—as in the Tipping Point—changes all this. Suppose one person is really "infected" with commitment for a change that is important for an organization's future. She spreads that enthusiasm to one person, yielding two people both with contagious commitment to this idea. Both of these people spread it to one more person *each*, giving four. Those four people can each infect one more each, giving eight. With every step the number of people infected with the new idea doubles.

Let's do a thought experiment on the power of doubling. Imagine a chessboard. On the first square, mentally place a single grain of sand. On the second square, place two; on the third place four grains. Continue doubling the number of grains in each square until all the 64 squares on the chessboard have been filled. How many grains of sand do you think would be on the chessboard? Most people guess around a 100,000 or sometimes as high as a million or two. The actual number of grains of sand is 18,446,744,073,709,600,000—or more than 18.4 quintillion.[vii] This is clearly a thought experiment. It is hard to imagine a number this big, let alone wonder how many miles of beach it would take to collect 18.4 quintillion grains of sand.

Even more interesting than this huge number is the fact that there are just slightly less than 4.3 million grains of sand on the chessboard when half of the squares (or 32 squares) have been filled. So when half the chess squares are filled, about two ten-trillionths of the total grains of sand would have been placed on the board.

Doubling the grains of sand on the chessboard is an example of exponential growth. Other examples include compound interest in a savings account or bacteria multiplying in a favorable culture.[viii] In these examples the increase with each step is not doubling. In a savings account, it is quite a bit less than doubling; the interest rate is usually quite small, but the result is still exponential growth.

The Power of Two Reveals Exponential Growth

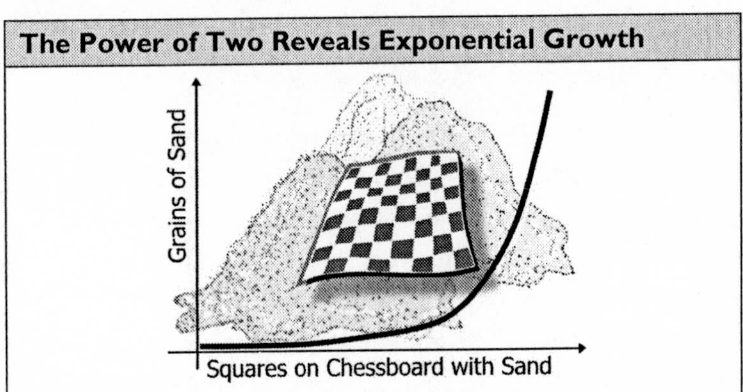

The Power of Two is an example of exponential growth, which always has the same characteristics. It begins slowly—at first appearing as if nothing is happening. In our chessboard example, the first square has 1, the second 2, then 4, 8, 16, and so on. At this rate, the first row contains 255 grains of sand. This is a manageable amount of sand. It hardly seems like a pattern that will lead to 18.4 quintillion. Yet once the tipping point is reached, the rate of growth expands rapidly—almost exploding.

Exponential growth starts out small and innocuous, but after reaching a certain point it expands very rapidly. This point is called the "tipping point." The characteristic of a tipping point is that the growth pattern changes. Before the tipping point is reached, the growth is slow; afterward the growth becomes rapid—increasing almost beyond belief. (See How Fast Is an Idea Spreading? on page 116 for a measure of reaching a tipping point.)

If a new idea or concept is in an environment where it becomes contagious, it reaches its tipping point, and only then do we begin to see rapid acceptance. In epidemics—whether the disease or the word-of-mouth variety—we never see the incremental step-by-step increase that is characteristic of linear growth. Rather the idea or innovation or change seems to appear to be going nowhere at first—and either it fizzles out or it suddenly reaches its tipping point and takes off.

In the right environment, organizational change can also spread exponentially. If each person spreads the idea to just one more person at a time, at first the idea spreads slowly, one person's enthusiasm spreading to two, those two spreading to four, then to eight. Sixteen seems like a very small number, but after a while it takes off—almost appearing beyond control—yet it always follows the same basic rule of *each* person spreading the idea to just one person at a time. Exponential growth comes from making the idea contagious and giving it potential for explosive expansion.

An Example: Internet Growth

Acceptance of the Internet and email saw exponential growth. Initially, few people outside the defense community even heard of email, then some major universities were included to facilitate joint research, then other universities, then businesses, and so on. When a critical mass was achieved, it grew beyond the imagination of the original developers.

Internet Growth

Out of cold war fears of losing technological superiority, in 1969, the U.S. government funded ARPA (Advanced Research Projects Agency) to research networked computers. By 1971, there were fifteen hosts connecting just a few ARPANet computers. NSF (National Science Foundation) got involved in 1984 by funding NSFNet to increase academic participation in the fledgling network begun by ARPA. By 1987 there were approximately 28,000 hosts in the network.

In 1994, the network was opened to communities and businesses who put more information on the Net. As more information was put on the Net, it became more valuable to its users—so more people wanted to be connected. The demand was huge and the growth of Internet hosts reached a tipping point and began to take off. In 1996 there were 9.4 million hosts. This soared to 105 million hosts by the end of 2000. The number of hosts is projected to pass 1 billion by early 2005.

There is a simple reinforcing loop driving the expansive growth of the Internet, especially after it was opened to businesses and individuals. As more information was put on the Net, more people wanted to be connected, so there was more demand for new hosts, so more hosts went online, which allowed more information and newer content to go on the Web so even more people wanted to be connected and so on. Thus the Internet fueled its own growth.

Reinforcing Loop Captures Internet Growth

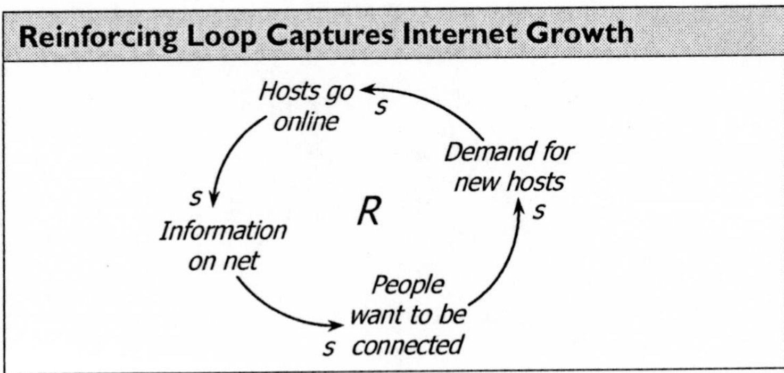

A self-reinforcing loop drives the expansive growth of the Internet. More information on the net increases the number of people who want to be connected, which drives the demand for new hosts; this creates the environment for more hosts to go online, which further increases the information on the Net.

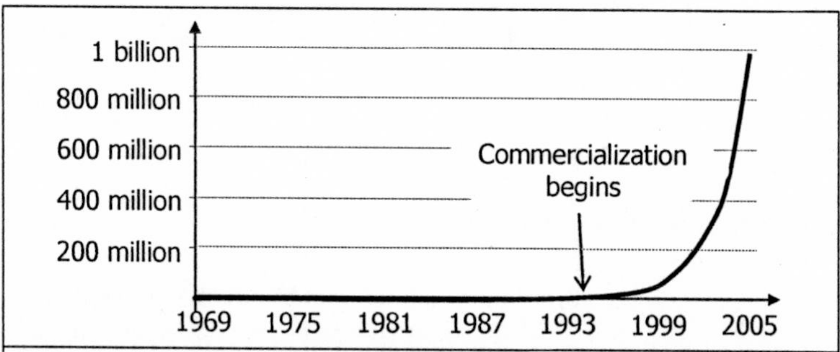

The plot of the exponential growth in the number of hosts is shown here. The plot clearly demonstrates a tipping point in the late 1990s, after commercialization. Growth was very slow before the tipping point and very rapid after it was reached.

When implementing change, we want to harness the energy of the power of two—recognize when it is happening and nurture it. Starting off so small and giving the impression that nothing is happening can be very discouraging. On the other hand, not everything that starts off small is exponential growth. A balancing loop with few and small delays also has very slow growth—especially as it approaches its asymptote. The lesson is to know the structure. Learn how the parts are interacting to give the dynamics that you are experiencing. Know what is causing the growth. If it is a self-reinforcing loop causing exponential growth, be patient and encourage it, especially if it is in the early stages. If it is a balancing loop reaching its asymptote, look for areas that you can change to help it take off. Ask yourself if you can you break the cycle of equilibrium and create a cycle of growth.

Later we will look at how the Tipping Point model is structured to help you leverage the exponential growth typified by the power of two. The Tipping Point shows how we can create exponential growth and tip an organization toward a needed change. First, let's look at "systems archetypes," which is the final systems thinking concept used by the Tipping Point model of change.

Spreading Commitment

> Never doubt that a small group of thoughtful, committed citizens can change the world. Indeed, it's the only thing that ever has.
> — Margaret Mead

Many of us can remember a time, well before DVD, when there were two competing videotape recording formats: Betamax (or Beta) and VHS. For a time it was not clear which format would become the standard for home recording. Today Beta is just a memory in a market dominated by VHS. Few experts would say that VHS is a superior product technically; in fact many professionals still use Beta. How did VHS come to be synonymous with home video recording? System thinking can shed some light on this. Through years of observation, system thinkers have noticed many patterns that repeat themselves in different contexts. They refer to these repeating patterns—and the structure that gives rise to them—as systems archetypes. The "success to the successful" archetype can help us see how VHS came to dominate the video recording market.

In the success to the successful archetype, two competitors seek a limited resource—in the Beta-VHS case it is the home video recording market. Each sale of a video recorder goes to one competitor or the other. If the sales for one competitor nudges slightly ahead of the other, then it gets more revenue. It can turn this revenue into development or marketing, which helps it get additional committed customers. Plus, supporting technologies go to the winner, making it easier to use. At the same time, the rival gets less revenue, making it less able to compete until it is squeezed out. In the case of Beta-VHS, each person who chooses VHS over Beta makes VHS more of a de facto standard for video recorders, giving it additional committed customers.

Success to the Successful Applied to Beta and VHS

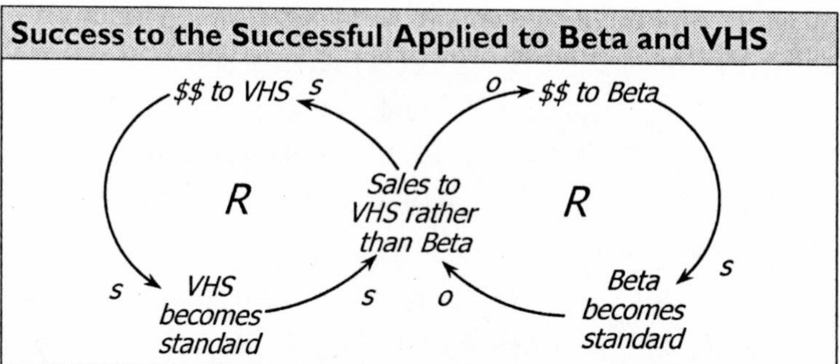

Beginning with the loop on the left, sales to VHS rather than to Beta result in more revenue to VHS. It uses this revenue to improve marketing and get more movies titles and thus become more of a standard. This increases VHS sales relative to Beta. At the same time, the loop on the right describes Beta. Revenues to Beta go down, because the dollars spent on video recording have a limit. This constrains its ability to market. So it becomes less of a standard and its sales relative to VHS go down even further.

VHS nudged the system in its favor initially by investing heavily in content, especially movie titles (whereas Beta put more emphasis on the technology). As customers bought VHS for the movie titles, it became more and more of a standard, relegating Beta to memory. Once the system gets nudged toward one competitor, then the old adage, "Them that gots, gets" succinctly describes the dynamics of success to the successful archetype.

Another way to think about this archetype is that the successful competitor's product becomes more valuable as more people switch to it. When one competitor nudges ahead of the other it becomes more attractive *because* it is more widely used. In this case, if more people are using VHS, new purchasers are more likely to buy it because they can exchange tapes with friends, they can more easily find prerecorded tapes, and so on.

The same archetype applies to an organizational change—as more people use the new process or tool or software or team-based skill, it becomes more valuable. Consider a Supply Chain Management (SCM) program that is designed to manage customer orders from sale to delivery. As more aspects of orders move from the legacy system to the SCM system, there is more information on the SCM system. When there is more information on the SCM system it is more useful, and so more people want their aspect of an order on the SCM system. The more the SCM system is used, the more useful it becomes. Once it gets started, the momentum swings more and more toward the successful competitor.

The More SCM Is Used, the More Valuable It Is

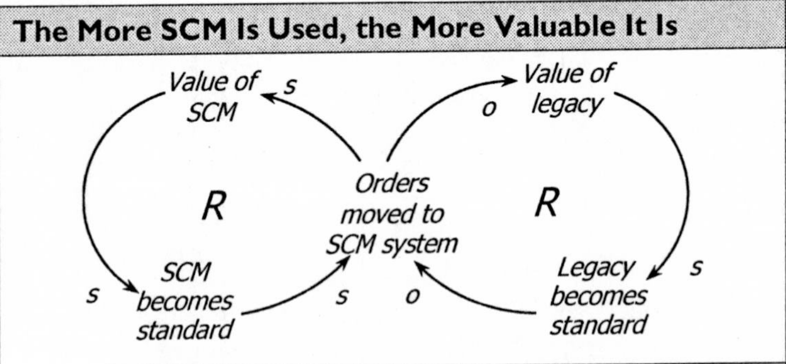

The structure driving the dynamics is captured in the diagram above. The key is that every aspect of the order process that moves to SCM makes the SCM system more valuable. Every aspect of the order process that is on SCM puts more information about individual orders on the SCM system. The same move makes the legacy less valuable. Eventually SCM becomes the standard—provided information is steadily moved onto it.

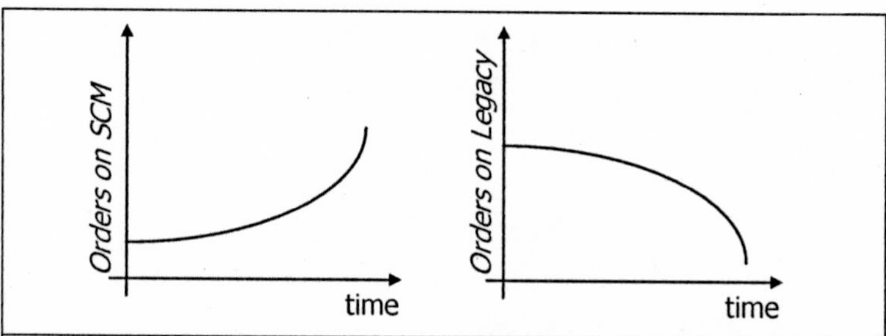

The dynamic behavior caused by this structure is captured on the two plots above. The number of orders on the SCM system begin low and rise while those on legacy begin high and drop.

Closing the Loop

An ancient Japanese proverb illustrates the limits of linear thinking and the value of thinking systemically. The proverb says, "When wind blows, the demand for wooden buckets goes up." Like many Japanese proverbs, it is very subtle. Here is what it means: When the wind blows, dust gets in the air. The dust gets in people's eyes and thereby causing some of them to go blind. In ancient Japan, blind people typically become folk-tale singers, who accompanied themselves using a shamisen, a guitar-like instrument made with cat skin. So as more people went blind, more cats were needed for the shamisens. So the number of cats went down. This caused the number of rats to increase. The rats like to chew on containers to see if there is anything good to eat inside. If they chewed on a wooden bucket, it became useless since it could no longer hold water. So people bought new wooden buckets—causing the demand to go up.

"When wind blows, the demand for wooden buckets goes up." —Ancient Japanese Proverb

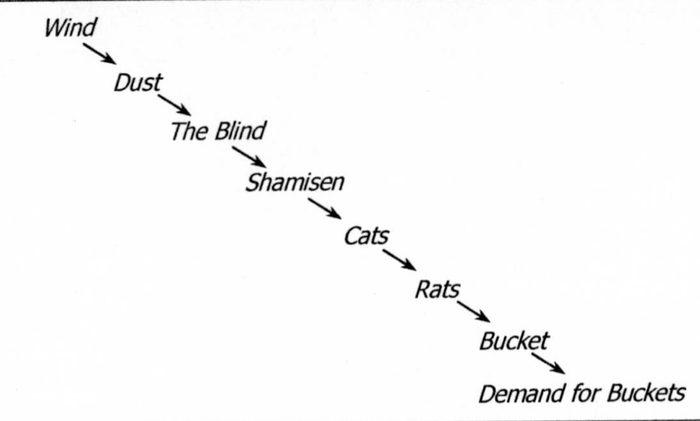

This is a linear representation. . . however, the system is *not* linear. We get a fuller picture by closing the loop.

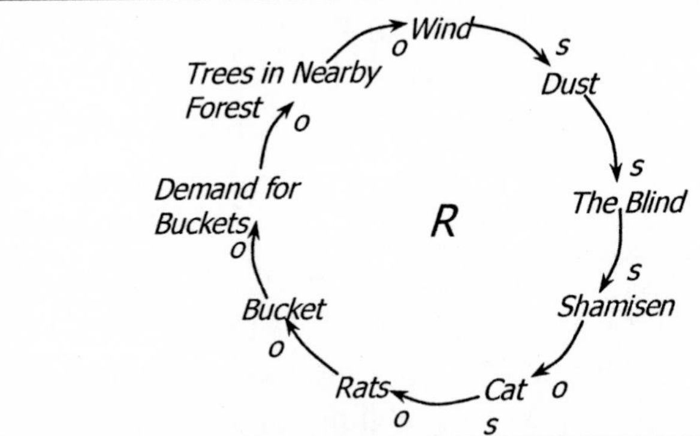

The linear thinking of the proverb misses the feedback that is captured in the systems view. In the systems view we see that wind increases the demand for wooden buckets, which causes people to cut down trees that protect the village. This actually results in more wind; it is a large self-reinforcing loop. The link-and-loop picture is richer and more accurate.

Of course we know that nothing can grow—or decline—forever. Systems thinking also tells us that there are more interactions and feedback loops to look for in this system.

Despite its subtlety, this proverb is quite linear. It fails to close the loop and reveal the larger context. What did wooden bucket makers do in ancient Japan when the demand went up? They went to the nearby forest, and cut down trees to make more buckets. With nearby trees cut down, the town was even less protected from the wind. So the town experienced more wind, so there were more blind people, fewer cats, more rats, and the demand for wooden buckets goes up further. The linear view of the proverb misses the reinforcing loop that is a huge engine of growth for wind and dust and blindness.

Systems thinking helps us think in wholes rather than parts and see the bigger picture. It provides a language to describe how parts interact to form wholes. It is part of what informs the Tipping Point model of change. The next chapter puts together the ideas from Chapters 2 and 3 to see what lessons learned from public health and systems thinking can teach us about how to spread an idea.

Moving Forward

Key Concepts

- The way of the systems thinker is to (1) think in wholes, rather than parts, (2) recognize the importance of time, (3) understand the effects of closed feedback loops
- The events that we experience are a result of system structure. All system structure can be defined in terms of balancing and reinforcing feedback loops. Balancing loops always create equilibrium, and reinforcing loops create exponential growth or decline.

- Systems archetypes are repeating patterns that we see in many different areas, which demonstrate the structure that drives events.

Points to Ponder

- What opportunities do you have to step back and see the bigger systemic picture? Can you create such opportunities?
- Are there aspects of your change that you are thinking of linearly that you could re-frame to find the feedback loops that drive it?
- How can you harness the power of two in your organizational change?

Chapter 4

A New Model of Change

The Tipping Point model stands out from other models of organizational change because it takes a dynamic view; it recognizes that change is a process that evolves over time. It goes beyond the static and linear approach typically seen in models of change by applying concepts from both public health and systems thinking. Its greatest strength is in recognizing that change happens when people change—when people's attitude toward an organizational change progresses from disconnected to committed. The Tipping Point relies and builds on the models outlined in Appendix 1: More on Models of Change, and it helps us see how they all fit into a dynamic, systemic picture of change implementation. The Tipping Point helps leaders understand the factors that create a positive epidemic of commitment and enthusiasm for an organizational change.

The Tipping Point Framework

> You cannot plan the future by the past.
> — Edmund Burke

The Tipping Point model focuses on the concept that each person's commitment to an organizational change can be contagious. Under the right conditions, contagious commitment can spread through an organization. Understanding the dynamic nature of the spread of contagious commitment gives leaders an advantage. They can better see their role, which is to create the conditions that foster contagiousness and thereby help spread important ideas throughout their organizations.

Like any model in business, the purpose of the Tipping Point is to improve results by improving implementation of an organizational change. The change may be designed to boost sales, upgrade processes, decrease costs, increase productivity, improve quality, reduce accidents, or otherwise enhance profits. To improve results, the Tipping Point concentrates on the most important aspects of creating contagious commitment. It provides the language we need to understand change implementation and highlights actions leaders can take in their organizations to make a change both contagious and sustainable. With a model that describes how change spreads in an organization, we are better able to make effective implementation plans, better able to discuss progress, and more likely to make strategic deployment decisions that move the change forward.

Much of the background for the Tipping Point has already been developed—in particular the four attitudes toward a given organizational change (advocates, incubators, apathetics, and resisters) as well as the two types of support: people and environmental support. This section reviews the attitudes toward change. It goes on to look more carefully at how leaders can engender people and environmental support—by introducing seven "levers of change." This chapter defines the levers of change and gives examples of using them. In the next chapter, we will take an even closer look at how the levers of change interact with each other—sometimes to create more leverage and sometimes in ways that can be dangerous.

Four Attitudes Toward Change Form Four Groups

As outlined in Chapter 2, at any point in time all the people in the organization fall into one of four groups or pools depending on their attitude toward the change. They are either infected by the change and are advocates of it, they have been exposed to the idea and are incubating it, they simply couldn't care less about it and are apathetic to it, or they are resisting it. Advocates have real experience with the change—this experience has demonstrated its value to them. Incubators have heard about the change, but they are not yet sure whether it will work or not in their situation. Resisters are pushing back against the change—either covertly or overtly. Apathetics feel disconnected from the change. Either they have not heard about it or do not believe that it will necessarily affect them. It is easy to underestimate the power of apathy and overestimate the effect of resistance. In a *Harvard Business Review* article, "Campaigning for Change," Larry Hirschhorn says that most change initiatives fail not from resistance or insufficient funds, but because people simply stop paying attention to them. They fail from apathy; they are ignored to death.

The people who are in each of these four categories or pools can and do switch categories. In the best of all cases you want to make all of them advocates of the change. You want to reach a critical mass (see page 53) of advocates so that the change reaches a tipping point and people flow naturally into the advocate pool. The following section examines seven levers of change, or actions that management can take, to influence how people's attitude toward the change evolves and thus what category they are in.

Four Pools of People in the Tipping Point Model
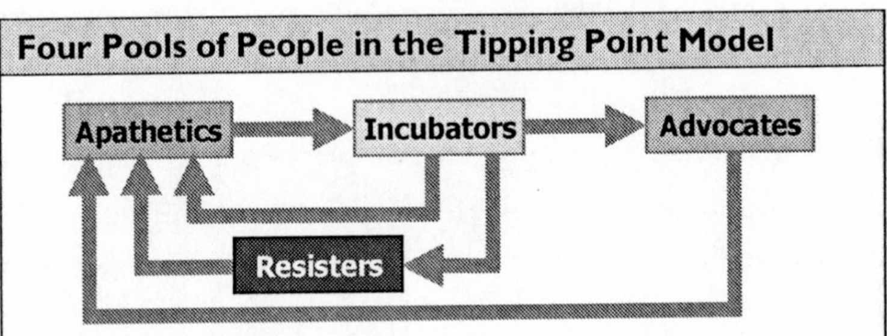
Advocates—Advocates are people with experience in the change who really believe that it will make a difference. They are interested in sharing their expertise and enthusiasm with others—in the hope of making the implementation of the change successful.
Incubators—Incubators are thinking about the change, but they are not sure if they believe that it will work or if management is fully behind it. They are thinking and learning about it and testing the concepts against their experience with work in their organization.
Apathetics—People are apathetic if they have not heard of the change or if they simply do not care. Based on previous experience, many people believe they can ignore a change and it will go away. Such people make up the apathetic pool.
Resisters—Resisters come in two varieties. Resisters who openly and actively challenge the change can be an important source of information. Their concerns may represent potential roadblocks that need to be addressed. On the other hand, people who are covertly undermining the change can be a dangerous hindrance to success.

Attitudes are contagious. A positive, committed attitude toward a change can spread from one employee to another—leading to effective implementation and the desired financial results for the organization. A negative, destructive attitude can also spread, with potentially disastrous consequences. Unfortunately, negative attitudes about the change tend to spread more easily than positive ones and can undermine even a change that is critical for your organization's success. Employees' attitudes toward an organizational change are affected by the perceived value of the change itself and by the support for the change. We can say that their attitudes are affected by the benefit or the burden that they believe that the change will bring and by the support, or perhaps indifference, for the change within the organization.

Perception of Value and Support Are Key Drivers

Management Support for the Change		Burden	Benefit
	High	Look for what caused the poor perception	Positive contagious commitment with potential to spread through the organization
	Low	Negative contagious apathy or resistance that leads to failure	Look for ways to increase the support, while there is still positive perception
		Burden	**Benefit**
		Perceived Value of the Change	

There are a number of factors affecting how employees perceive the value of a change initiative. These include the value that it will bring, their own experience with change initiatives in the past, what their co-workers are saying about it, and the level of management support for it. Even when the perceived value is high, it is important to back it up with strong management support for the change.

The perceived value of a change and the support interact in predictable ways. A change perceived as a benefit to an organization that is well supported will obviously be the most likely to succeed. At the opposite end is a change that is perceived as a burden (even if it has potential to be a benefit) and is not well supported by leadership. Such a change is almost certainly doomed. The negative attitude toward such a change is sure to spread quickly through the organization. If employees perceive a change as worthwhile but don't see it supported, then it is important to find ways to increase the support for employees to make the change. If the change is perceived as a burden—find out why. It could be a valid and fixable problem with the change itself or the business case needs to be made more clearly. The table on the previous page shows the four situations when perceived value and support interact.

"Fair process" is defined by Kim and Mauborgne in an article in the *Harvard Business Review.* Attending to fair process can give a positive bearing to people's perception of the burden or benefit of a change. Their research has shown that "individuals are most likely to trust and cooperate freely with systems—whether they themselves win or lose by those systems—when fair process is observed." In short, people tend to be as concerned with the fairness of the process as the fairness of the outcome. Kim and Mauborgne have defined three principles of fair process—*engagement, explanation,* and *expectation clarity. Engagement* refers to involving people in decisions that affect them and encouraging discussion and examination of assumptions. Management still has the responsibility of making the decisions, which is where *explanation* comes in. Everyone affected by a decision should understand the reasoning behind it. Once the decision is made, there are new rules and *expectations.* It becomes management's responsibility to make these new expectations clear. Fair process is not consensus or majority rule. It is involvement, sincerity, and transparency, and it can influence employee's perception of the value of a change.

Recall Medical Machines, the firm from Chapter 2, Applying Lessons from Public Health, that developed a new product line in response to competition from start-ups. The sales force lacked experience with the new products, so Medical Machines implemented knowledge management (KM) system in an attempt to overcome poor communication between sales and engineering. At the same time that Medical Machines was implementing the KM system, it was involved in another organizational change. Medical Machines had to maintain their standard of attracting and retaining the most talented employees. As people with different backgrounds entered the workforce, the pool of potential new employees endowed with the skills that Medical Machines needed was becoming more diverse. To present a positive work environment for this new talent, it recognized the need to increase its own diversity.

A Diversity Initiative at Medical Machines

There were two main business drivers of the diversity initiative at Medical Machines as well as two smaller motivators. First, the demographics of the new employee pool were growing more diverse (becoming more variable in gender, race, country of origin, and sexual orientation). If Medical Machines expected to both attract and retain the most talented people from this pool, they needed to present a positive work environment for them. Second, the face of their customers was changing. In Medical Machines' traditional market, hospitals were also drawing their new hires from the same diverse talent pool. So customers who were making the buying decisions on medical test equipment were more diverse. At the same time, Medical Machines was selling more globally, further increasing the diversity of the customers. There were also two smaller motivators for the diversity program—one reactive and one proactive. On the reactive side, the firm supplied medical test equipment to military and veterans hospitals, and it feared that in the future the government might impose quotas on them. On the proactive side, many managers within Medical Machines recognized that diverse teams simply outperformed homogeneous teams. Diverse teams represented many different viewpoints and thus more creativity.

The director of the diversity program understood the importance of advocates, so she formalized the advocate network. She created a description of the skills, interests, and experience she felt were needed to advocate for a "flexible, inclusive, motivating environment for maximum contribution." People actually applied to join the formal advocate network. Advocates were asked to give 10% of their time to the network, so coordination and buy-in from their management was clearly required. Almost 40 of the over 100 employees who applied were accepted into the network. The group met initially for a five-day residential training. To get the information needed to accomplish the vision, they heard from experts in racism, gender, sexual orientation, foreign customs, and language differences as they applied to business. They got training in being proactive, identifying and dealing with problems, as well as team building. To continue their support, there were monthly advocate teleconferences to keep people together, share success stories, and deal with challenges. The advocate network named themselves "strategic termites," because their goal was eating away at the dead wood of wrong-headed ideas on diversity so that new ones had room to grow.

Resistance to the diversity program was a definite reality. One source of resistance came from executives who did not understand the business case and confused the initiative with compliance to governmental mandates. To overcome this resistance the diversity director enlisted the help of a senior vice president of sales who thoroughly understood and realized the significance of the business case. He had been with Medical Machines for many years, during which time he established a successful reputation in sales and marketing and was responsible for some key accounts. Because he was a white male, most of the executive team could identify with him, and they felt they understood his motivation. He put himself on executive team meetings' agendas to lay out the business case for diversity. He spoke privately with peers on the changing face of the customer and listened to their concerns. Before long, everyone on the executive team understood the business case, and resistance at the executive level was greatly reduced, if not eliminated. Dealing with this major barrier early on was important to their success.

Resistance at lower levels of the hierarchy was just as real. There were several approaches used to address this resistance. The first approach centered on constant honesty. Frankness and candor describing the problems of a homogeneous workforce and the long road to attaining diversity were key. Further, it demanded honestly admitting mistakes in implementation and demonstrating a willingness to rectify them. A second approach to removing resistance involved managing expectations. It is not unusual for diversity programs to expose problems that have affected performance, but were hidden. Exposing these problems is part of addressing them; however, it can make things appear worse before they are better. Everyone needs to be educated to expect this "worse before better" outcome, which is common to many change initiatives. (See page 48.) The third method was more direct. In some departments, diversity criteria in hiring, promotion, and education were added to managers' goals and used in their annual reviews. This raised awareness. It also reduced resistance when managers also fully understood the business case.

Turning apathetics into incubators was mainly done through contact with members of the strategic termite network of advocates, but other methods were also used. These efforts focused on keeping diversity on employees' "radar screen" and giving them information on what to expect. The advocates offered voluntary, day-long courses in diversity. The Medical Machines company newspaper was peppered with articles on the value that diversity brought to the business and on executive commitment to it. Over time this resulted in growing numbers of advocates, some of whom eventually joined the strategic termite network.

We can see that all four attitude pools were represented in the diversity initiative at Medical Machines. To make the initiative stick, management's challenge was first to create the environment in which most people fully perceived the value that it could bring. Next they had to support the change so that people would become advocates of it and it could spread. The seven levers of change, described next, are the means to create this informed, supportive environment.

Levers of Change

> There is nothing more powerful than
> an idea whose time has come.
> — Victor Hugo

The Tipping Point examines seven actions, called the seven levers of change, that management can use to produce support for a given change. These levers are fairly generic; they represent a wide range of related, specific actions that management can take to affect people's attitude toward the change and their willingness to embrace it. The levers fall into two categories—people-support and environmental-support levers. The four people-support levers are contacts between advocates and apathetics, mass exposure, hiring advocates, and removing resisters. The three environmental-support levers are walk the talk, reward and recognition, and infrastructure.

The Tipping Point's Seven Levers of Change	
People Support	***Environmental Support***
• Contacts between Advocates and Apathetics • Mass Exposure • Hiring Advocates • Removing Resisters	• Walk the Talk • Reward and Recognition • Infrastructure
People-support levers directly affect the flow between pools, whereas environmental-support levers are equally important but less direct. The idea of people moving or flowing between pools is fundamental to the Tipping Point structure, so an analogy of pouring wine from a barrel might be useful to understand the distinction between people and environmental support levers. People-support levers are like a spigot; they directly affect the flow. The more that you open a spigot, the faster the flow. Environmental-support levers are like tilting up the barrel; it changes the environment so that for the same spigot position, there is more flow. We could say that opening the spigot has a direct effect on the flow, and tipping the barrel is changing the environment to affect the flow more indirectly.	

These actions are called levers of change because just as a lever and fulcrum give a mechanical advantage when used properly, these seven levers of change give an implementation advantage when changing an organization. The specific actions under each lever vary from organization to organization and from change to change. For some organizations a particular lever may be very powerful and another counterproductive, but for every change all seven levers must be considered.

People-Support levers

People-support levers directly affect the flow of people from one attitude pool to another. Two levers affect the flow from apathetic to incubating: contacts between advocates and apathetics as well as mass exposure. Contacts are opportunities that advocates have to share their experience and enthusiasm for the change with people who feel disconnected from it. These are often casual one-to-one meetings in the hallway, but they can include more formal town-hall meetings. The key to contacts is that they must provide two-way communication between the advocates and apathetics. This distinguishes contacts from mass exposure. Mass exposure refers to introducing the change by using posters, splashy Web pages, mass emails, one-size-fits-all awareness training, or other means designed to make people conscious of the change. Mass exposure typically does not provide for any feedback from the people who are the targets of the change. Neither of these levers guarantees that people's attitude will change from apathetic to incubating, but they have the potential to affect people's attitude—each in varying degrees.

The other two people-support levers are hiring advocates and removing resisters, which affect the flow into the advocate pool and out of the resister pool, respectively. In business, hiring and attrition are going on all the time. The hiring advocates lever represents hiring that is over and above hiring people for skill or succession or growth. People hired via this lever are hired specifically because they are advocates—because they have expertise, experience, and enthusiasm for the change. For example, a firm implementing an enterprise resource planning (ERP) program to manage orders, manufacturing, and order fulfillment hired people from a related industry who had experience with the ERP. These new employees provided expertise customizing the ERP to the specific needs of the company, but they would not have been hired had the firm not needed them specifically for their expertise in ERP.

There is one final lever of change on the people side: removing resisters. Resisters are pushing back against the change. It may be necessary to move resisters to a department that is not affected by the change, to give them assignments more consistent with their beliefs, or perhaps to remove them from the company. Removing resisters can also include changing the implementation plan so that groups that are resistant will be affected after the change's value is established. I worked with a team who decided to change their rollout plan for a new payroll system to affect union members later in the schedule. After working with the Tipping Point simulation, the team felt that the union would feel more supported—and be more supportive—if they saw success with the new system in other areas and knew that they were not the guinea pigs for a new system.

Examples of the Four People-Support Levers
Suppose we are implementing a customer relationship management (CRM) system. CRM systems maintain historical and current customer data. Well-designed CRMs provide for better customer service and improved sales by providing detailed customer data available to the employee who needs it. The following could be examples of the four people-support levers of change in implementing a CRM.
Contacts between Advocates and Apathetics—There are a number of ways that advocates could share their experience of a CRM with those who are apathetic. For example, effective salespeople with experience in CRM can explain how the information on customers that was available in the CRM database helped them make sales. Or customer support people can explain how it helped them find trends in problems re-

ported by customers that made them more effective at supporting customers.

Mass Exposure—A CRM would probably require general awareness training so that everyone knew what it meant and basically what to expect. A Web page with more detail could supplement the training. Articles in the company newspaper with examples from other companies or divisions on the benefits they realized with CRM would be useful. Including some fun stuff like logo mugs might also be helpful, but only if it is matched by serious environmental support.

Hiring Advocates—Hiring an advocate of CRM who came from an unrelated business who would not normally be hired for skill or succession or growth might be necessary, if it is done prudently. For example, a company with no CRM expertise might hire people with knowledge in the technical side of implementing a CRM, even if their experience is in a different business.

Remove Resisters—If the sales force is resisting the change, begin the implementation with customer service. After the resisters see the value that a CRM offers, they are more likely to come on board. If a key leader is among the resisters, it is vitally important to understand why and address the source of the resistance if possible or remove the person from the key position. If you cannot change people's attitude to embrace the change then it may be necessary to work with different people.

Environmental-Support levers

Environmental support is as important as people support; without it even a very important change for an organization is likely to fail. The Tipping Point looks at the effects of three key environmental-support levers of change: walk the talk, reward and recognition, and infrastructure. *Walk the talk* refers to leaders leading by example. Leadership means setting the standard, or in Mahatma Gandhi's words, a leader must "be the change" that he or she wants to see. In the Tipping Point model, walking the talk is the percentage of opportunities the leaders have to exemplify the change that they actually take advantage of. For example, taking every opportunity to make the business case for the change clear is walking the talk. On the other hand, trying to lead a quality initiative without including quality metrics in product development reviews is not. Other examples of walk the talk are monitoring progress and making course corrections. A leader who is serious about a change will not only *take* every opportunity to model the change, he or she will *craft* more opportunities.

Reward and recognition includes monetary incentives as well as formal and informal recognition in support of the change. The range of rewards and recognition is broad. It includes financial rewards like raises, bonuses, or stock options. It includes formal recognition and awards as well as an informal thank-you note or a public pat on the back. Rewarding and recognizing individuals and teams who support a change gives focus to the importance of the change to the organization. As a lever of change, reward and recognition can be thought of as the proportion that all the rewards and recognition depend on implementing the change. Obviously, a firm needs to reward and recognize many things. So the proportion of the reward and recognition that is devoted to a given change should reflect its importance.

The last environmental-support lever is *infrastructure.* Every change requires some sort of infrastructure. This could include hardware, software, facilities, processes, manuals, and so on. Infrastructure will be different for each change. For example, merging business units could require changes to compensation policies, new HR policies and manuals, and perhaps focused job-specific training to help the two business units understand each other's product lines or processes. Implementing a supply chain management system could require different infrastructure, such as software and workstations. There is always an ideal amount of infrastructure to support a change. However, in the real world, there are budget constraints, so we are forced to make decisions about how much of the ideal we are willing to invest in.

A participant in a Tipping Point workshop described a very clear example of the reality of investing in less than the ideal amount of infrastructure. She was working with a Fortune 100 company that was doing a major overhaul to its benefits package. Investing in 100% of the ideal infrastructure would mean purchasing an expensive automated call distribution (ACD) system as well as many new workstations for the human resources (HR) staff, which was responsible for answering questions about the new benefits. After the benefit system was implemented, the new ACD and workstations would no longer be needed. The firm's management felt that they simply could not justify the expense for infrastructure that had such a short shelf life, no matter how valuable it was during the implementation. Instead they invested in a comprehensive Web page that could answer many employees' inquiries and would remain useful after the implementation was completed. The Web page reduced the number of calls to HR asking for particulars on the new benefits plan, but did not eliminate them. Without the ACD, employees got more busy signals when calling HR than the firm wanted. In the end, the solution was less than ideal, but they felt it was much more cost-effective.

Examples of the Environmental-Support Levers

Continuing with the CRM System example (from page 103), the following could be examples of the three environmental-support levers of change.

Walk the Talk—There are many ways to lead by example with a CRM. For example, clarifying the business case to all stakeholders and creating buy-in for the CRM is walking the talk. Making sure that company systems (i.e., compensation, operational reviews, business strategy) are aligned with the CRM is also walking the talk. Making sure everyone hears about instances where the CRM was a benefit to the company. Encouraging use of the CRM over the legacy system whenever possible.

Reward and recognition—Rewards include raises and bonuses for both implementers and users of the system. There are many ways to give recognition. One example is handwritten thank-you notes to implementers or formal awards for people who use the information documented in the CRM in novel and useful ways.

Infrastructure—Every CRM needs customized software and perhaps hardware. There is also probably job-specific training so that people know how to use the CRM tools effectively. Job-specific training is tailored to a person's responsibilities, so that the sales force would get different training than the customer service staff. (This is in contrast to the generic training that is part of mass exposure.)

The Levers of Change and the Pools Interact

The salient question is: How do these seven levers interact with the four attitudes that employees may have toward the change? First consider the people-support levers; these have a direct effect on the flows of people between the attitude-pools. Contacts with advocates and mass exposure have the *potential* to move people from apathetic to incubating. Under the right conditions, they can change people from feeling disconnected from the change to thinking about its effect and the power it may have. This is not to say that both levers are equally effective or that neither has side effects, but they both have a potential to move apathetics into becoming incubators. Hiring advocates provides a second entry into the advocate pool. (But it is laden with side effects, which we'll get into later.) People can enter the advocate pool from inside the company through incubation or they can enter from outside through hiring. Removing resisters has the immediate effect of reducing the numbers in the pool of resisters (though, like hiring advocates, it can also have other less desirable side effects that we will see later.)

Environmental-support levers create the atmosphere to support the change. In essence, they make the people-support levers more—or less—effective. For example, if the environmental support is high, then people tend to spend less time incubating the change before getting the experience needed to become advocates. Similarly, high environmental support makes contacts between advocates and apathetics more effective (which is more likely to result in incubation). It mitigates some of the undesirable side effects of hiring from the outside. In general, environmental-support levers provide the underpinning that makes the change work.

In addition to the three levers of change, there is one more factor affecting environmental support. This factor is the population mix itself, that is, the ratio of advocates to apathetics. In an organization with many advocates, it is easier to remain an advocate. Advocates learn from each other and provide a mutual support network. On the other hand, a lone wolf, a solitary advocate, is likely to either return to the apathetic pool or perhaps even leave the company. The population mix is part of the context that can be either conducive or not toward an organizational change. Thus, it is the fourth input to environmental support, but it is not a lever of change because it does not represent an action that leaders can take to effect change.

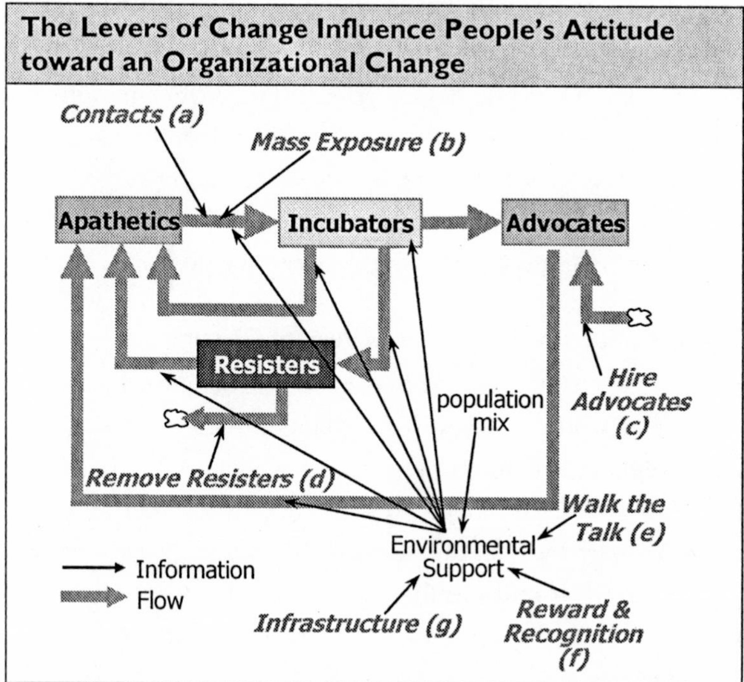

The Levers of Change Influence People's Attitude toward an Organizational Change

The seven levers of change in the model are: (a) the number of contacts between advocates and apathetics, (b) mass exposure to the new idea, (c) infusing new advocates through hiring, (d) removing those involved in resistance, (e) leaders walking the talk, (f) reward and recognition, and (g) providing infrastructure, such as equipment or other support. Levers a–d directly affect the flow of people between the attitude pools and are people-support levers. Levers e–g are called environmental-support levers because they affect the context for the change.

The previous diagram adds the seven levers of change to the diagram on page 94 of the four attitude pools. In it, you can see the major effect of each lever. For example, you can see that contacts and mass exposure affect the flow from apathetic to incubating. You can see how the three environmental-support levers as well as the population mix affect environmental support, which in turn mediates most of the other flows between pools.

The following chapter describes all the levers in more detail and considers how they interact with each other, and some of their side effects. Before going into depth on the interactions, let's spend a bit of time examining the major effects and how the levers affect people moving between the pools.

Major Effects of the Seven Levers of Change

To begin with, you could think of the people who are advocates in the early stages of a change initiative as the very early originators in terms of the change styles outlined by Musselwhite. (See Critical Mass beginning on page 53.) They are eager to share their enthusiasm for the change. They have experience with it and see the value that it has for radical improvement. They talk with people who are apathetic. Some of the apathetics will begin to incubate the ideas behind the change. While incubating, they begin go through the transition stages described by Bridges, (See Models of Change on page 15 or for more detail Appendix 1: More on Models of Change.) They begin letting go of their old ideas about how work gets done and begin considering new ones. They have to deal with the ambiguity of giving up very familiar ways of working while being unsure of precisely what the new ways will be like, how effective they will be, and so on. Incubation cannot be rushed. It takes time to consider the value of new ideas. It takes time to learn and try out new processes. This is all part of incubation.

Remember that employees can move from apathetic to incubators in a second way—through mass exposure. Attending a class or an information session or reading a mass email or poster will cause some apathetics to think seriously about the new change initiative. It is unlikely that the same proportion of people will begin incubating after mass exposure as do after contact with an advocate. On the other hand, most mass exposure can reach more people at once. These people will also begin the transition process described by Bridges, which initiates the incubation process.

Once people have become incubators, they can do one of three things: (1) They can say to themselves, "this isn't for me, not in this organization," and go back to the apathetic pool. (2) The change can resonate with their experience and values so they become advocates. (3) Some of the incubators may begin to resist the change, believing it to be counterproductive or inconsistent with their beliefs or how they view the organization. Which of these paths that the incubators take depends on the environmental support for the change—more support tends to make more advocates. Further depending on the support for the change, resisters may continue to resist or they may become apathetic again.

It is important to remember that advocates cannot be taken for granted. Initially, advocates' own enthusiasm may mask a lack of sponsorship for the change. (In *Managing at the Speed of Change*, Daryl Conner outlines this trap, and there is more on it in Appendix 1: More on Models of Change.) However, without a sponsor backing an organizational change, it is unlikely to succeed. So if advocates doubt the sponsorship, evidenced by a lack of environmental support, then they may decide that there is no real advantage for them to stay behind the change. In such a case, they would tend to go back into the apathetic pool or leave by attrition.

The story of Serious Software that began in Chapter 1 helps illustrate the levers of change in action. Recall that Serious Software developed customized software for doctors, dentists, and other professionals. The firm had enjoyed a reputation for nimble response to customers' requests, but it was beginning to erode due to quality problems. To improve software quality, it introduced a new step called code inspection into the design process. This final installment on Serious Software illustrates how the seven levers of change were used—or in some cases misused.

Quality at Serious Software . . . Concluded

The designers, testers, and first-line managers who were affected by code inspections recognized the importance of quality. A few of these employees had done code inspections in previous jobs at other companies, and were advocates of the value that code inspections could bring to quality. However many more of the targeted employees believed that the testing process was a better way to improve quality than code inspections. Some of them became vocal resisters, pointing out deficiencies with how code-inspection data were being used. Most people were apathetic; they felt like bystanders to a new fad from management.

Let's look at how Serious Software used the levers of change to create advocates of code inspections. First consider the people-support levers at Serious Software. The company invested in training for everyone affected. Designers, testers, and first-line managers all attended the same standardized, general training that concentrated on the value to expect from code inspections. This training created a substantial pool of people incubating the possible value that code inspections could bring to quality. Training was only part of a huge mass exposure effort. Besides training, they distributed pencil cups with code inspection logos on them and fancy pen sets for everyone involved. While there were a number of advocates, they were not identified so there was no attempt to leverage their expertise or enthusiasm. Resistance was ignored—even when it came from those managing designers expected to implement code inspections. In sum, Serious Software's people support was limited to the mass exposure campaign.

Their implementation of the environmental-support levers also left quite a bit of room for improvement. First, let's consider infrastructure. Like most quality efforts, to be effective code inspections require a fair amount of data collection and analysis. Thus, tools to collect and analyze the data made up most of the infrastructure needs in the code inspection initiative. The firm failed to provide any tools or automated ways to collect, collate, and analyze the data. There were designers, probably the early advocates, who actually created such tools on their own. They made the tools available to others, at least to those who knew that these tools even existed. The company did not attempt to standardize the tools or distribute them or recognize these designers for their early spontaneous efforts.

Their track record with rewards and recognition and walking the talk was not much better. Many line managers were good about rewarding designers from other groups who participated in inspections for designers in their own group. However, this practice was not organized or practiced uniformly. Further, the leadership did not track any of the code inspection statistics in their biweekly status reviews, nor did they add any time in the schedule for designers to accomplish code inspections, which were an extra step in the design process. This lack of infrastructure, poor recognition for extraordinary efforts, and lackluster walking the talk quickly soured the target population.

Code inspections had clear business value for Serious Software, and there is an interesting postscript to this story. After about two years of very limited application, the firm was ready to give up on consistent application of code inspections. At the same time Serious Software needed object-oriented (OO) software designers for a large project. They hired a large number of new university graduates for their OO skills from large engineering schools. These universities also happened to be ones with software engineering programs. So these new grads were taught that code inspections were part of the design process, and they expected to do them as part of their jobs. These new hires sought out the existing tools, and they pressured for more and better tools. They reported quality metrics in status reviews—whether or not they were required by management—which led to more rewards for good code inspectors.

By hiring these programmers, Serious Software accidentally hired a large number of advocates, but they were not hired because they were advocates. They were hired for skill and growth, so they did not cause the side effects that usually accompany hiring from the outside just for the change. (These side effects are described in more detail in the "fixes that fail" archetype on page 130.) These new designers' expectations eventually tipped much of the design community toward accepting code inspections as part of the design process. However, properly supported, the change could have been accomplished at Serious Software in one design cycle, in less than one year, and without the influx of these new designers. Instead, full implementation dragged on over several years, nearly failed, and impacted many design cycles—with the corresponding financial consequences.

Had they understood the Tipping Point model of change, Serious Software could have implemented code inspections with much less pain. The leaders would have realized that over time the attitudes and actions of the people in the organization change, depending both on the change itself and on the support for it. Leaders would have recognized their role to balance the seven levers of change to create an environment that fosters the spread of commitment toward the change. Change is a process, so the "right" values for the organization and for the change will vary as the implementation progresses. Balancing the levers to create the environment conducive to change demands constant attention and willingness to adjust.

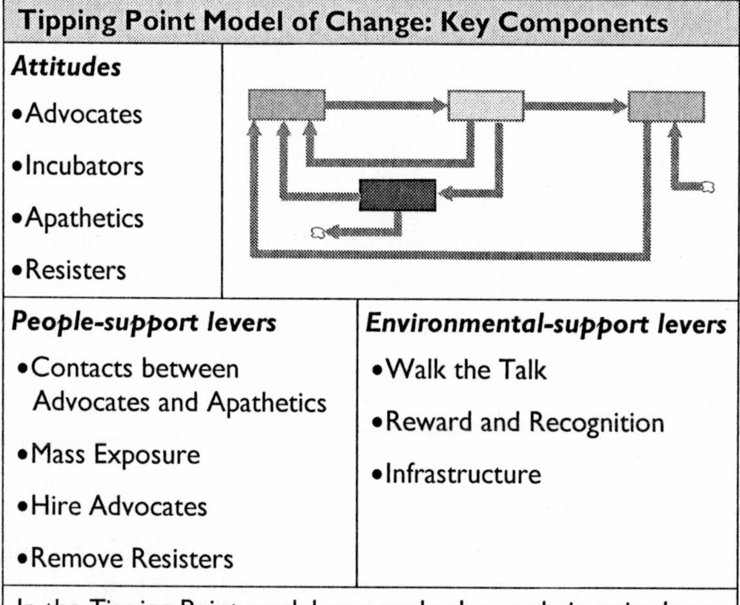

Tipping Point Model of Change: Key Components

Attitudes

- Advocates
- Incubators
- Apathetics
- Resisters

People-support levers

- Contacts between Advocates and Apathetics
- Mass Exposure
- Hire Advocates
- Remove Resisters

Environmental-support levers

- Walk the Talk
- Reward and Recognition
- Infrastructure

In the Tipping Point model, as people change their attitude toward the change they switch between pools. Managers need to use the seven levers of change to move the entire organization into the advocate pool. This demands attention to how the levers interact.

Earlier (on page 34), we considered Gladwell's explanation that the spread of an idea was the result of content, carriers, and context interacting. In the Tipping Point model, content is the inherent value of the change. It is the value-add to the business of implementing this new way of doing work. Carriers are the advocates of the change. Context is influenced by the seven levers of change. Used with attention to their interactions, the levers can create a context conducive to change.

How Fast Is an Idea Spreading?

> Success is never final.
> — Winston Churchill

Imagine that your brother-in-law just inherited a state-of-the-art sports club. He wants to increase profit by increasing membership. By initiating a huge new membership drive, he might fall into the trap that many sports clubs have fallen into. He would offer huge incentives to his sales staff to sign up new members. He'd put his focus on bringing in new members without even investigating what would make his existing members renew their dues each year. This would leave him with lots of new members, few renewals, and huge expenses for advertising and incentive programs.

It is an easy trap to fall into. We see mobile phone service and long distance providers doing it, too. It also happens in change management. It is so easy just to focus on getting new advocates for a change. However, if these new advocates are not supported, they become former advocates—very quickly. This causes a double whammy. It forces the organization to spend time and energy and money to get new advocates. At the same time it means that the advocate pool has less experience with the change. So they have less expertise to share with others, lowering their overall effectiveness as advocates.

Keeping the tipping ratio in mind is a way to avoid this trap. The tipping ratio is simply the ratio of new advocates to former advocates. A short thought experiment helps illustrate it. Suppose you have 1000 advocates for a particular change. If 100 new people become advocates each week and 100 people lose interest (and all other things are held equal), then it is easy to see what would happen with this idea over time. The size of the advocate pool would remain the same. There would be different advocates, but the number of advocates would be the same. The tipping ratio would be 1.0.[ix] If 99 people become advocates and 100 people lose interest, then the tipping ratio would be 0.99 (that is 99 new advocates divided by 100 former advocates) and the advocate pool would slowly dwindle to nothing. If 101 people become advocates and 100 people lose interest, then the tipping ratio would be 1.01. The change will spread (all other things being equal), but it will spread fairly slowly. However, if the same 99 or 100 or 101 become advocates and only 1 loses interest, then the tipping ratio would be around 100 and you would have created a positive epidemic of change that will spread very quickly. If the ratio is above 1, then the idea is spreading; if it is a lot greater than 1, then the idea is spreading very rapidly.

The tipping ratio is an instantaneous measure of how fast an idea is spreading. Sometimes we get trapped into just thinking about getting new converts, new advocates. The purpose of introducing the tipping ratio is not to create a new metric; rather, it is to remind us that getting new advocates is not enough. An idea spreading in a population depends just as much on taking care of those who already believe in it and know that it's useful. So it's not just creating more advocates; it's also supporting, encouraging, and keeping up the enthusiasm of the people who are already advocates.

Using the Tipping Ratio

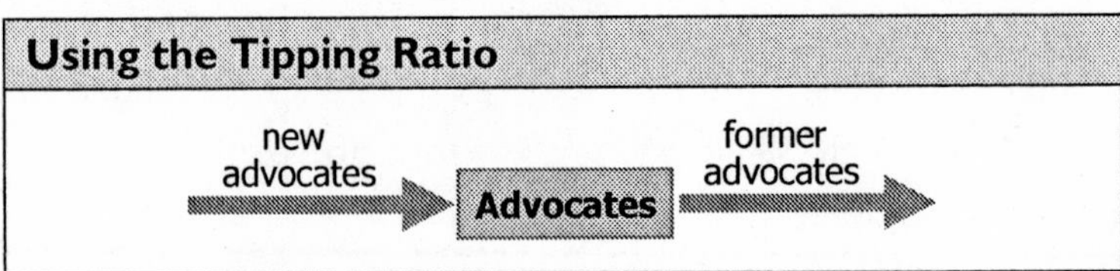

The ratio of people entering the advocate pool to those leaving it is called the tipping ratio, thus:

Tipping Ratio = (new advocates/former advocates)

Charles Dickens's character Mr. Micawber understood the tipping ratio. In *David Copperfield* he said, "Annual income twenty pounds, annual expenditure nineteen and six, result happiness. Annual income twenty pounds, annual expenditure twenty pounds ought and six, result misery." The same lesson applies to organizational change, if more people become advocates than leave the advocate pool, then the system will eventually tip toward advocates.

Micawber's formula, though, yields very slow savings. Organizations cannot wait that long. To be successful with organizational change, we must get the tipping ratio way above 1 *as early as possible*—and keep it there. We need many more new advocates than former advocates. The way to do this is by supporting and thus keeping the existing advocates as well as creating new ones.

We can paraphrase an adage from marketing to underline the importance of the tipping ratio. There are three objectives to successfully implement a change: (1) get advocates, (2) keep advocates, and (3) grow advocates. The tipping ratio speaks to getting and keeping advocates—both are absolutely fundamental to spreading a change within an organization. It is also important to constantly develop the advocates' capacity to advocate a change. Review the section on Advocate Skills (page 59). The more skillful advocates are at spreading the change the better their morale and the more effective they will be at spreading acceptance for the new organizational change.

Moving Forward

Key Concepts

- The dynamics of the Tipping Point model result from recognizing that people's attitude toward a change initiative evolves over time. The Tipping Point takes into account four stances people may have toward a change initiative. (1) Advocates—people with experience, expertise, and enthusiasm toward the change. (2) Incubators—people who are trying to understand its effects. (3) Apathetics—people who feel disconnected from the change. (4) Resisters—people who oppose the change, either overtly or covertly.

- Leaders can foster change by using seven levers of change: (1) contacts between advocates and apathetics, (2) mass exposure, 3) hiring new advocates, (4) removing resistance, (5) leaders who walk the talk, (6) rewards and recognition, and (7) investing in infrastructure. Levers 1–4 directly affect the advocate-apathetic mix and are people-support levers. Levers 5–7 are called environmental-support levers because they affect the context for the change. Levers interact to help—or hinder—adoption of change.

- The tipping ratio reminds us that it is as important to support existing advocates as to bring new ones on board. In fact, there are three objectives to successfully implement a change: (1) get advocates, (2) keep advocates, and (3) grow advocates.

Points to Ponder

- Are you in a position to leverage hiring so that people who you hire for skill, succession, or growth also happen to be advocates of your change?
- Do you have a plan for examining all seven levers for applicability to the change in your organization? Remember that examining for applicability leaves open the possibility of rejecting any that don't apply to your particular change, but only after they are considered carefully.
- Do you have a mechanism to see how many advocates of your change you are getting and keeping?
- Can you leverage informal networks to form a community of practice of advocates so that they can collaborate and learn from each other?

Chapter 5

Dynamics of the Tipping Point

There is no prescription for change. All the levers need to be considered. For any given change, some levers need to be addressed and used in concert and others are just not appropriate. This chapter spells out how to use the Tipping Point model as a framework to understand how to make better decisions about using the levers. This chapter begins with a closer look at the levers and how different change initiatives influence how the levers are put into practice. The chapter contrasts the systemic viewpoint provided by the Tipping Point with the linear view that dominates most mental and formal models of change. The chapter ends with two systems archetypes that are used to explain some of the important dynamics captured in the model.

Levers of Change in Action

> Give me a lever long enough and a fulcrum to place it on, and I can move the world.
> — Archimedes

Applying the Tipping Point model, requires understanding both the levers of change and the types of actions that exemplify each lever. In this section, we go into more detail on the levers and examine how they interact. Not all levers are equal. Some levers can be powerful, but also present a serious danger if overused or underused. Other levers are useful in one situation and counterproductive in another. Most levers give more bang for the buck when used together. This section introduces these interactions, and they are developed further in the subsequent section, Traditional vs. Systemic View of Change. Let's begin by looking at the people-support levers: contacts between advocates and apathetics, mass exposure, hiring advocates, and removing resisters.

Contacts between Advocates and Apathetics

Contacts between advocates and apathetics are essential to spreading acceptance of and commitment to an organizational change. There is no substitute for the firsthand experience that advocates have. Their experience allows advocates to really explain the value of the change. It is their credibility combined with their enthusiasm that is contagious. There will always be some spontaneous contacts with advocates and apathetics, but there are ways to leverage advocates and ensure more contacts. One way is through town-hall meetings that provide a forum for advocates. These are not just information sessions. Town halls must be designed to encourage real dialogue. Participants must feel safe to air their concerns; management must be willing to let these concerns have an effect on the deployment, when it is appropriate. This honest and open exchange is essential to effective contacts.

Another good way to facilitate contacts between advocates and apathetics is by identifying and using the formal and informal networks and relationships between people and departments (see more under Weisbord in Appendix 1: More on Models of Change). Informal networks provide a natural space for employees to discuss problems they have encountered and learn about appropriate ways to handle them. Working within these social networks can be a very powerful way to spread ideas, because the networks are made up of people who value and trust each other's opinions. Creative leadership finds ways to leverage the natural connections between advocates and others and to form further connections.

Another way to cultivate contacts is to include advocating the change as part of each advocate's responsibility. Be careful not to overdo it and take focus away from real work, because it undermines advocates' credibility. If they spend too much time advocating, they will begin to talk to the same people repeatedly or they will burn out. Worse yet, they will be seen as *just* advocates for the change and lose their credibility as someone with expertise in the product or service that the company produces—thereby becoming less effective as advocates.

Whichever way contacts happen—informally or formally, one-to-one or one-to-a-few, spontaneously or planned—the strength of contacts is in providing a forum for two-way communication. Contacts are an opportunity for apathetics to hear about the change from someone with experience in it. They provide a way for apathetics to get more clarification and to raise issues that they may have with the change. This two-way communication is what distinguishes contacts from mass exposure.

Mass Exposure

In many (perhaps even most) organizations, mass exposure is the most overworked lever of change. Every form of mass exposure has been used to promote a change, including posters, mugs, T-shirts, mass emails, splashy Web pages, and so on.

Perhaps the most overused—or over abused—form of mass exposure is the one-size-fits-all awareness training. This is not training that helps one learn the specifics of how one's job will be done under the change. Awareness training just gives people an overview of the change or sometimes the value it is designed to bring. In general, training becomes mass exposure when it is one-size-fits-all. When everyone, independent of his or her job or how he or she will be affected by the change, goes to the same training, then it is mass exposure. For clarity, it is important to contrast awareness training with job-specific training that gives employees the skill and the information that they need to do their job under the new way of working. Job-specific training is an aspect of infrastructure.

Organizational change implementers sometimes confuse mass exposure with communication. *Communication* shares a Latin root with *common* and *community*. By definition, communication is participative. It is two-way; it involves both sending and receiving information. Ideally, in communication both sides can learn from listening to each other. In contrast, mass exposure is typically one-way; information is imparted from those "who know" to passive listeners who are supposed to just soak it up. Even if there is time or a venue for questions, the answers tend to be superficial.

I once worked with an organization that was devising a communication plan for the rollout of a new risk assessment process. The entire plan was mass exposure, including glitzy screen savers, video monitors constantly playing outside the elevators, special newsletters, and T-shirts. There was not a single opportunity in this communication plan for the leaders to learn from the people affected by the change. There was no attempt to leverage the expertise of people familiar with the process. The communication plan was exercised—despite my dissent. It was met with a collective yawn from engineers who were expected to implement the new risk assessment process. This lack of enthusiasm resulted in a six- to nine-month delay in implementing the process, not to mention wasted money.

Mass exposure is not communication. It is simply a way to expose people to a change. Confusing it with communication inevitably leads to expecting more from it than it can deliver, which is what happened with the risk assessment process. Mass exposure has its place in supporting change. If it is backed up with solid environmental support, it can be a cost-effective way to create awareness about a change. It cannot do more than create awareness; relying on it to do more is ineffective at best and likely to result in more cynics than advocates of the change.

Hyping a Change Initiative

A manufacturer with a large share in a regulated marketplace was instituting a customer-mandated quality program. This manufacturer had built its reputation on its ability to respond quickly and to add features to meet customers' needs. Its responsive reputation was being drowned out by quality problems, which were visible to both customers and regulators. To continue to enjoy its market position, the manufacturer began a quality improvement program with a huge kickoff, inviting customers and employees. The mass exposure program created real awareness of the quality program and the value that it could generate. Employees were interested in increasing quality, but few really knew what was expected of them. No new processes were put into place to improve quality.

In the subsequent few weeks there was more mass exposure. Everywhere one looked, there were posters, T-shirts, mouse pads, and coffee mugs with the quality program logo.

Hardly a week went by without a mass email extolling its value. Employees were all required to attend a course on the general quality practices. Professional speakers presented at lunch-and-learn sessions to inspire employees to value quality. Yet there was no supporting infrastructure to gather and use metrics to improve quality. There were no rewards for improving quality. There was no training in the specifics of how to reduce variation and improve quality in their own jobs.

Before long, employees recognized that the media campaign was just happy talk because the manufacturer was not backing it up with strong environmental support. They lost interest. Over a year later, the quality program had hardly gotten off the ground. It was abandoned, which adversely impacted the manufacturer's market share.

A systems engineer recounted a mass exposure experience that she had while working at a company implementing a six-sigma quality program to improve their product development process. She was required to attend a three-day training program that she called a sheep dip because the ideas taught were so narrowly focused that they were irrelevant to most people in the class. Very little of the course material could be applied to the everyday decisions that she made in her job. However, there were some advocates among the students. These people were respected peers with similar responsibilities but in a different geographic location. They knew how to get work done at their company and understood and valued six sigma. Because of these advocates, class participants had some useful conversations, sometimes in class but often during the breaks. She found these discussions constructive, and they gave her an appreciation of six sigma that she did not have before. Even more important, after the class was over, she found the advocates to be excellent thought partners to help her apply the analytic techniques from the course in her daily job responsibilities. In her words, "Mass exposure leavened with advocates can rise and even become a positive thing."

Some mass exposure is almost always necessary. However, because it is tangible and can be planned, controlled, and implemented as a stand-alone project, it is very easy to overdo mass exposure. Worse yet, when the first media campaign doesn't work, or when its effect wears off after a few weeks, it is not unusual to follow it up with a larger one. The "shifting the burden" systems archetype captures these dynamics of mass exposure. Shifting the burden is a systems archetype that depicts the situation where greater and greater dependency is put into a symptomatic fix (like mass exposure) at the expense of applying a more fundamental solution. It gives insight to prevent a major pitfall of mass exposure.

Suppose you realize that many employees see the change as the flavor of the month, so if they ignore it, then it will go away. A fundamental approach to address this skepticism would be to demonstrate value from the change as well as management's full support for it. This approach includes Kotter's advice to create, measure, and report early wins (Appendix 1: More on Models of Change) and also includes rewarding those responsible for them. However, these actions take time. It is easy to believe that there is not time for this type of fundamental approach. A huge media campaign, which makes people more aware of the change and could include information on why it is needed, is much quicker.

A media campaign can affect employees' beliefs that the change will stick. However, focusing on a media campaign draws attention and management support away from the on-the-job demonstrations of value. This leaves people wondering about the need for the change, which can further turn up the heat on the media campaign. More focus on the media campaign draws even more resources and focus away from the on-the-job demonstration of value. Appreciating the pervasiveness of the shifting the burden archetype provides leverage to counteract this trap. If we see overdependence on mass exposure, it is time to break the cycle. It is time to really emphasize producing early demonstrations of value and making sure all concerned have heard about them.

Shifting the Burden: The Danger of Mass Exposure

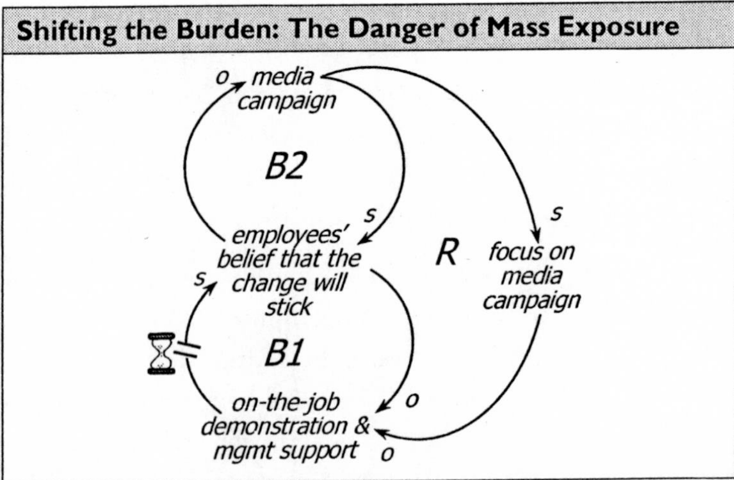

Shifting the burden recognizes that a problem can be addressed in two ways, either by a fundamental or a symptomatic approach. We may realize that a more fundamental solution would be better in the long term, but time pressure often drives us toward the more symptomatic approach.

The more we apply the symptomatic solution, the more resources we draw away from the fundamental solution. The burden of solving the problem is shifted away from the fundamental toward the symptomatic one.

In this case, the low level of *employees' belief that the change will stick* is the problem that needs to be addressed. Both a *media campaign* (symptomatic approach shown in B2) and the *on-the-job demonstration of value & management support* (more fundamental approach shown in B1) will affect the employees' belief that the change will stick.

It takes time to create the *on-the job demonstration of value & management support* (B1). The *media campaign* is quicker, so we usually start with it (B2). However, if we don't demonstrate the value of the change, then the effect of the *media campaign* will wear off. Worse yet, it draws resources and focus away from *on-the job demonstration of value & management support*—further eroding *employees' belief that the change will stick* (R). This, in turn, leads to further stoking up the *media campaign.*

Ultimately the burden of affecting employees' belief that the change will really stick shifts away from the more fundamental demonstration of value toward the media campaign.

Hiring Advocates

Sometimes it might be necessary to hire advocates from outside the company to accomplish a change—especially if you completely lack the necessary expertise in house. However, hiring from the outside needs to be done very judiciously. If too many people are hired from the outside, resentment builds up against them. Everyone has heard complaints like, "They just don't understand our culture" or "No one ever listens to anyone from inside." This resentment, by association, spreads to the change itself. "Fixes that fail", another systems archetype, can shed light on the problems with hiring advocates. It describes the situation where applying a fix that might help things in the short term actually makes the situation worse in the long term.

Let's look at how the fixes that fail archetype captures the pattern of hiring advocates from outside and thereby creating resentment that reduces the number of advocates in the long run. Suppose you realize that your population mix just has too many apathetics and too few advocates or you completely lack the expertise for the change. You might choose to hire some advocates from outside the company. These are people that you would not have hired otherwise—for skill or succession or growth. They are hired just for the change initiative. In the short term this puts more advocates in the pool and improves the population mix. However, if you hire too many people from the outside it creates resentment inside. This resentment can lower the effectiveness of mass exposure and also cause more incubators to regress back to being apathetics. What we see is that the short-term fix—especially when overused—can make the situation worse in the long run.

Fixes that Fail: How a Short-term Fix Can Hurt

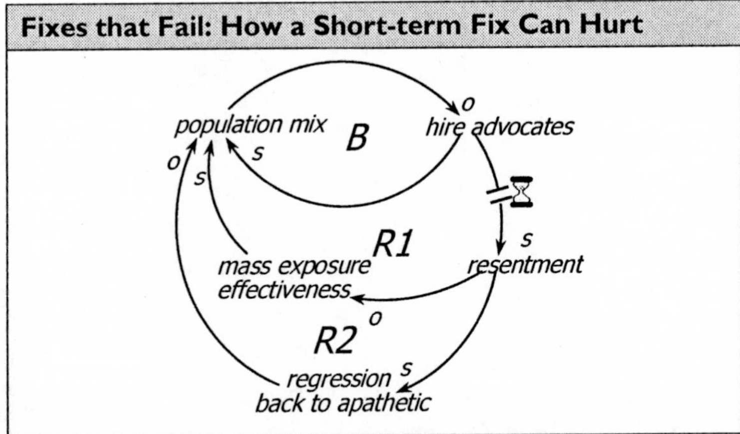

You apply a fix because you want results, but sometimes all you get is consequences, because it is the very fix that makes the situation worse. The basic lesson from fixes that fail is that the fix that works in the short term can make the situation worse in the long term.

Suppose we realize that the *population mix* has too few advocates in it. So we hire advocates from outside the company to raise the proportion of advocates. Hiring advocates helps the *population mix* in the short term (B). However, if overdone, it creates *resentment* that makes other efforts less effective. In particular, people are less likely to pay attention to the message from the mass exposure (R1) so *mass exposure effectiveness* goes down, and they are less likely to move from incubation to advocates so *regression back to apathetic* goes up (R2). Thus, in the long run hiring advocates actually makes the proportion of advocates in the population mix lower.

The lesson of fixes that fail, in this case, is to be very judicious about hiring from the outside. Be convinced that it is absolutely necessary. When you must do it, be sure that you also create opportunities for existing advocates and even incubators, to help mitigate the negative side effects.

Removing Resisters

Resistance to change is probably inevitable. Dealing with this resistance can be a very difficult proposition in any change. It can be tempting to believe that all resistance is bad. Daryl Conner (see Appendix 1: More on Models of Change) distinguishes between open and covert resistance. Covert resistance is dangerous and can undermine a change initiative. In contrast, open resistance can be healthy and even make a change more successful. An organization that allows, or even encourages, its employees to openly discuss problems and issues that they have with a new initiative is more likely to discover potential glitches early in the process, before they become serious obstacles.

Resistance can be damaging, but how it is dealt with can have a greater effect on a change effort than the resistance itself. If a resister is in an influential position, it is important to know the source of his or her resistance. If this concern is not something that can or should be addressed, it might be necessary to move the person to a less influential position or to a position less affected by the change or perhaps even outside the company. With less influential people, just waiting them out is often the best solution. As the change becomes more successful, their voices will be drowned out by the success. If it is necessary to remove resisters, timing is critical. If most of the population is apathetic toward the change, then removing a resister will appear arbitrary and can lower morale. On the other hand, removing a resister from a population with many advocates for the change sends a clear signal to them that the change is supported.

Now let's consider the environmental-support levers: reward and recognition, infrastructure, and walk the talk, and what actions leaders can take to affect them.

Reward and recognition

Reward and recognition as a lever of change represents the percentage of reward and recognition that depends on implementing this change. Rewards are the typical monetary rewards—salary increases, bonuses, stock options, and so on. Recognition can range from a simple "atta-boy" to a handwritten thank-you note to a formal award. Senior leaders who fail to use the power of their position to recognize a job well done are missing a huge opportunity. A straightforward, sincere thank-you note can be a very valuable, and cost effective, way to recognize an employee that can engender a strong sense of collaboration. Whatever form of reward and recognition used, it is important to identify the key tasks that must be accomplished to create the change. Timely rewards for doing those tasks are an important lever of change.

The most effective rewards and recognition link desired decisions, actions, and behaviors, either of teams or individuals, to business results. Such incentives reinforce the business case behind the change and demonstrate a clear commitment to it. Look for behaviors and decisions that are required to make the change work. Then reward or recognize the business results that come from those behaviors and decisions.

Infrastructure

Infrastructure refers to a class of actions that management can carry out, such as providing job-specific training, tools to capture and disseminate lessons learned, or a well-defined roll-out plan, as well as tools, software, or processes that are specific to the change itself and to measuring progress. Each change will require different infrastructure, but typically there is some infrastructure necessary for every change.

A few examples give a sense of the potential range of infrastructure and show that different organizational change initiatives require different infrastructure. To implement a quality program in manufacturing, infrastructure would include tools for capturing variation, statistical programs for keeping track of the variation, and possibly computers to run those statistical programs. To implement a supply chain management program, such as SAP, the obvious infrastructure is software and workstations. Further, infrastructure would include targeted training that teaches people how to do their jobs under the supply chain management system. (This is different than one-size-fits-all awareness courses that are really mass exposure.) Infrastructure can also include the so-called soft stuff. For example, whether we are building a learning organization or implementing SAP, we need to adopt new processes, improve information flow, foster skills such as dialogue, improve communications with customers and suppliers, and build effective teams. For an initiative to understand customer needs better, infrastructure could be the tools that market research teams and human factors teams need, like prototyping equipment and surveying instruments. Other examples of infrastructure needed to get closer to the customer could be aligning sales compensation and information systems to the initiative. A huge change on the scale of merging two business units could require all sorts of infrastructure. It might require internal infrastructure such as a call center to help employees understand the new structure. It would probably need customer-facing infrastructure like a reorganized sales team to sell the combined products from the business units. Last, implementing computer-based training for the sales team would likely require infrastructure such as servers and courseware, because the sales team is typically on the road. Of all the seven levers of change, infrastructure is probably the most varied and the one whose specific execution is most tied to the particular needs of the change itself.

Walking the Talk

Walking the talk, or leading by example, is a vital environmental support variable. Any change to an organization presents its leadership with real opportunities to lead by example. The key opportunities include making sure everyone understands the business reasons behind the change, clarifying the vision and expected end state, paying attention to results, and making course corrections as necessary. Walking the talk can be measured by the percentage of opportunities the leaders have to lead by example that they actually take. In his book *Leading Change*, John Kotter describes eight important steps to walking the talk that are outlined in Appendix 1: More on Models of Change.

All too often organizational changes are seen as something to fix the employees, so leaders fail to see their own role in the change. They become skilled at talking the walk, at using the buzzwords associated with the change, but not integrating it into their actions. However, failure to lead by example sends a very clear signal of lack of commitment toward the change. Nothing speaks louder about management's resolve toward a change than seeing him or her leading by example. One of the most important ways a leader can walk the talk is to make the case for the change crystal-clear and make sure that all those affected understand the value of making the change successful and the consequences to the business of not doing so. On the other hand, there are countless ways that a leader can undermine a change. For example, trying to lead a supply chain management (SCM) initiative but looking to the legacy system for familiar reports is just talking the walk. It sends a clear signal that the SCM initiative is not important and undermines the prospect for success.

An effective leader has a clear vision of what the changed organization will be like and takes every opportunity to articulate it so that all stakeholders share in the vision. Without a clear vision, a change is doomed; the everyday demands that employees face will overwhelm a vaguely defined change initiative. Once the vision is established, it remains important to evaluate progress toward the goal. This implies being close enough to operations to recognize small wins or make course corrections, if necessary. Without a clear vision and constant monitoring of progress an organization is just flirting with a change and is unlikely to succeed. The following story illustrates a leadership team, which began by walking the talk, but did not build a clear vision of what the end state would look like and failed to monitor progress enough to recognize when the situation went awry.

Lacking a Clear Vision

A company with a diverse consumer product line had enjoyed substantial market share for many years. The firm was beginning to see its market share erode, and leadership feared that they had gotten out of touch with evolving consumer needs. They launched a program to understand and anticipate changes in the personal care market. The leadership did an excellent job of creating a burning platform (that is making the consequences of not changing so clear that no one could ignore them). As a result, everyone understood why the company needed to understand consumer needs better to stay in front of the competition.

Realizing the importance of empowerment, the leaders drove the responsibility of implementation down to middle-level managers. However, they did not provide a clear vision or framework of what they expected. This resulted in turf battles among the market research, human factors, and sales teams. Each felt better equipped to understand consumer needs and thus drive the effort. These turf battles put significant drag on the program. They moved the focus away from creating a better understanding of consumer needs to focusing on which team could dominate the others without challenging its own ideas on consumer needs. Had the end state been more articulated by the leadership, or they had been closer to the action, these turf battles could have been avoided.

Recall from page 37 that Meg Wheatley and Myron Kellner-Rogers counsel that a leader's role is to create connections, provide information, make resources available, and then let the organizing processes work. This is the heart of the leader's role, but I believe there is more. The leader must establish the goal and motivate people toward it, by making the end state very clear and establishing the dangers of maintaining the status quo. Their job is also to monitor progress and remove roadblocks. If progress is not what it should be, it could mean returning to either of the leader's first responsibilities. It could require returning to reestablishing reasons for the change clearly to all stakeholders. Or it could possibly require improving connections, information, and resources. This road map for walking the talk is illustrated in the following diagram.

The Roadmap for Walking the Talk

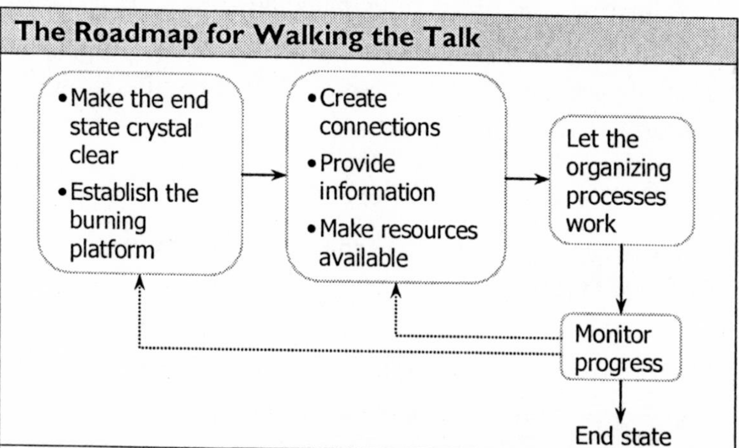

The leader or sponsor of a change must establish the desired end state and make the road clear for change by creating connections, providing information and making resources available. The organizing processes are very powerful, but the leader must also monitor progress. Sometimes it is necessary to return to one of the first two steps. Given the complexities of the modern organization and of changes we undertake, it is nearly impossible to plan every step in advance. Returning to an earlier step is not a failure. It is the result of good due diligence and will likely lead to continual improvement.

In a *Sloan Management Review* article, Orlikowski and Hofman argue against the traditional model for managing change, in which the major steps are defined in advance and the organization follows those specified steps on a specified timeline. In the turbulent environment in which most companies find themselves, such a model is less useful than a more flexible model of change—especially when implementing technology that must be adapted to the organization's needs. They argue for an improvisational model of change, which fosters experimentation, feedback and corrections along the way. Such a model allows the organization to take advantage of "evolving capabilities, emerging practices, and unanticipated outcomes." In fact, they argue that if you examine them carefully, successful change initiatives are already following the improvisational model, even while they claim to be using the more traditional approach.

People-Support and Environmental-Support levers Working Together

The people-support and environmental-support levers combine to create the context for change. All of these seven levers of change can be carried out in many different ways—depending on the change and on the organization.

Reviewing the Levers of Change

The ***people-support levers*** of change directly affect the numbers in each pool directly by influencing people's attitude toward the change and thus how they flow between the pools.

Increasing ***contacts*** betweens advocates and apathetics occur when more people who have experienced the value of the change to their own jobs get a chance to talk about their experience with people who are apathetic.

Providing ***mass exposure*** refers to one-size-fits-all training or a media campaign to get people aware of the change and provide a general exposure to the change and its value.

Hiring advocates refers to hiring people—who would not otherwise be hired—who are knowledgeable and have experience and enthusiasm for the change and thus become part of the advocate pool.

It might be necessary to ***remove resisters*** to another area unaffected by the change or change their assignments or remove them from the company, but only after their concerns have been heard and addressed when necessary and appropriate.

The ***environmental-support levers*** of change affect the level of support in the environment for the change.

Reward and recognition includes financial incentives, such as raises and bonuses, as well formal and informal recognition, such as thank-you notes and awards, that depend on successfully implementing the change.

There is a wide range of ***infrastructure*** such as job specific training, tools to capture and disseminate lessons learned, a well-defined deployment plan as well as tools, software, or processes that are specific to the change itself.

Walk the talk represents the percentage of time that the senior management is leading by example, which includes making sure everyone understands the business reasons behind the change, clarifying the vision and expected end state, paying attention to results, and making course corrections as necessary.

None of these levers of change is a panacea by itself. Depending on how they are used, they can create a context that helps or hinders an organizational change implementation. Their impact comes from how they interact with each other. All the levers need to be addressed or considered and used in concert. The following account describes using the levers together to advantage to accomplish a change that was necessitated by a situation thrust on a firm by external circumstances.

Using the Levers Together

A large high-tech company had an organizational change imposed on it when two of its largest customers merged. The two customer companies had very different reputations, corporate cultures, and approaches to business. The biggest change within the high-tech company was the effect on the two account teams who served these two customer companies. Each account team reflected the values and the processes of their respective accounts. No one, not even people in the customer companies, knew which corporate culture the merged company would reflect.

The high-tech company prepared for inevitable changes in the merged company. An account executive was appointed with experience on both account teams and who was respected by both teams. His task was to create a new account team to serve the newly merged company. His new account team had to serve the customer during their own transition and be ready to continue serving them irrespective of which corporate culture emerged. He began his tenure with a description of the challenges and changes ahead, which was clearly spelled out to both account teams.

The new account executive commissioned a study of the strengths of each account team and their view toward the company that they had not served pre-merger. Every salesperson's opinions were heard. The account executive made himself responsible to promote contacts between sales people who recognized the importance of being ready for any eventuality in the merged company and those who maintained a bias for the culture of their own premerger client. An informal knowledge base was created to help the two teams get acquainted with each other and with their respective customers. He was careful to structure financial rewards to support cooperation between the teams and to ensure the merged company's success. He dealt quickly with problems, removing salespeople who were so entrenched in one culture as to be unable to work with the merged account team.

In terms of the Tipping Point levers, he typified walk the talk—sending a clear message that the change was important and why. There was some mass exposure, but it was limited to providing information. Contacts with advocates, removing resisters, infrastructure, and reward and recognition were all used in concert. Hiring advocates was not needed, and it was not used. As a result, the high-tech company benefited from a productive relationship with the merged customer company for many years. By all traditional measures, such as sales, profits, and customer relations, the organizational change was successful.

The account executive realized the high stakes when two major customers merged, and he had enough organizational savvy to realize that no single lever of change was going to move his new account team to successfully serving the newly merged company. His proactive approach—using six of the seven levers together—helped ensure success.

Traditional vs. Systemic View of Change

Seek simplicity, and distrust it.
— Alfred North Whitehead

In their best seller, *The Fifth Discipline Fieldbook*, Senge, Ross, Kleiner, Roberts, and Smith argue that natural languages, such as English, influence our understanding of cause and effect. Subject-verb constructions help us understand "A causes B," but cloud our understanding of "A causes B and B causes A" (such as we saw in the systems archetypes in earlier sections). Thus, natural language construction (especially among Western languages) leads us to think of actions as being one-way rather than part of a feedback loop. Further, there are delays in most cause-and-effect relationships, and some delays have a significant effect on the outcome, but everyday language lacks a good mechanism for talking about the effect of time. This leads to a view of change in which independent actions have an independent effect on the outcome, which in a change initiative is the number of advocates.

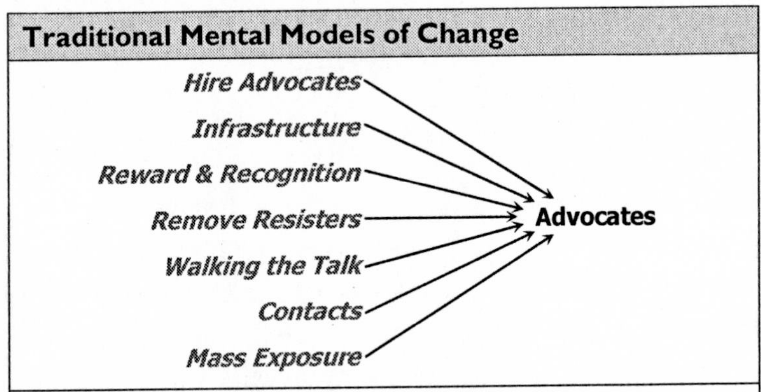

Traditional Mental Models of Change

Possibly because of the way that language is structured, mental models of cause and effect are like this diagram; each lever of change has an independent, one-way effect on the outcome. Most statistical models have the same structure. We do not inherently have a language of links and loops to help us think through the long-term effects as well as the interactions between variables. Systems thinking is designed to provide such a language.

This linear, feed-forward structure reflects the difficulty that we have to think through the feedback loops that are inherent in most of our actions. This picture is in contrast to the dynamics captured in the Tipping Point model. Many of these dynamics are captured in the diagram on page 109, and additional important interactions and their consequences are described in the following section.

Dynamics of Change

You can observe a lot by watching.
— Yogi Berra

Interactions between the levers of change and the population groups makes organizational change difficult to manage and accounts for its less than stellar success record. This section outlines some of the important interactions and feedback loops. These interactions are placed in four categories to make them easier to remember. The categories are: (1) What goes around, comes around. (2) Combinations matter. (3) Not all levers of change are equal. (4) Apply the "Goldilocks test" to any lever of change. At the end of this section there is a diagram of the Tipping Point model that adds these interactions and updates the diagram on page 109.

What Goes Around, Comes Around.

There are a number of self-reinforcing loops inherent in organizational change. An overarching one involves the population mix, which is the ratio of advocates to apathetics. Stated simply, the more advocates there are in the population, the more friendly the atmosphere is to accepting even more advocates. More specifically, recall that the population mix is one of the factors in environmental support, which affects the flows of people between each pool. When environmental support is high, more people will flow out of incubation toward advocate; whereas if it is low, they flow back toward apathetic. These flows in turn affect the numbers of people in each pool, which affects the population mix. So as the population mix goes up, it increases the flow toward the incubation and advocate pools and away from the apathetic and resister pools. This will tend to drive the population mix up further up. The reverse is also true. If the population mix goes down (that is, favors apathetics) then the flows toward incubation and toward advocate will go down. This will drive the population mix even further down. So the population mix ultimately reinforces itself.

Similarly, the environmental-support levers of change all reinforce each other. This happens because all of them drive environmental support up and all of them are more effective when the environmental support is higher. For example, walk the talk raises the level of environmental support, and so do rewards and recognition. Furthermore, rewards are even more effective when there is walking the talk, and walking the talk is more effective when there are rewards. This applies to all three environmental support variables—they each reinforce each other.

Let's consider walk the talk and reward and recognition in implementing a customer relationship management (CRM) system. When leaders are setting the example by walking the talk and using the reports from the new CRM system in sales reviews, then the environmental support for the CRM goes up. When environmental support is higher then the bang for the buck of each dollar invested in reward and recognition for the implementation team is greater, its effect on environmental support is greater. Higher environmental support, in turn, makes the effect of seeing those CRM-based sales reports in action even more significant.

The following example can help illustrate how the environmental-support levers are self-reinforcing. It is a story about a missed opportunity—about a company that could have leveraged more from their environmental support.

Making Environmental-Support Levers Work for You

A public health research firm wants to expand the base of clients they serve. To help implement this change they give substantial bonuses to employees who win research grants in new areas. However, they do not facilitate grant writing with supporting infrastructure or leadership. They have not been particularly successful at getting the new grants they need to increase their client base.

The bonuses would have greater effect if they were combined with infrastructure and vice versa. The firm could increase the infrastructure support by targeting employees with proven ability to write winning grants and support them with time to write, clerical staff, sending them to conferences, and so on. This would encourage employees to take the risk of writing proposals for grants in new areas to earn the bonus money. If grant winners are rewarded by bonuses and other recognition, these employees would become advocates and encourage others with the ability to write winning grants. Leaders who walked the talk by clearly articulating the business case for grants would further increase the environmental support, making the infrastructure and bonuses more effective. Together all three environmental-support levers could be used to create the atmosphere to win the grants and increase their client base, in a way that bonuses alone cannot.

Combinations Matter

Most levers of change are more effective when used in combination with others and some are even dangerous when used alone. Mass exposure, hiring advocates, and removing resisters are three variables that should never be used alone. Consider mass exposure. Some mass exposure is necessary, but it can be easily overdone and create cynicism. However, when it is combined with high levels of walking the talk and infrastructure and with appropriate reward and recognition, then it is more effective and less likely to create cynicism. Similarly, hiring advocates from outside the company can create the resentment that drives the fixes that fail archetype, described on page 130. The likelihood of creating this resentment drops with greater environmental support.

Similarly, as mentioned before, the effect of removing resisters depends on the proportion of advocates and apathetics in the population mix. If advocates are in a small minority, then removing resisters appears arbitrary and thus has a negative effect on environmental support. On the other hand, if the population mix tends to favor advocates, then removing resisters demonstrates that the firm is serious about the change and thus has a positive effect on environmental support. These negative effects can be mitigated and the positive effects enhanced by using the three environmental-support levers.

Not All Levers of Change Are Equal

Some levers are essential, and I call these must-have levers of change. Other levers should only be used judiciously, since they have the potential to be counter productive. Contacts between advocates and apathetics and walk the talk are must-have levers. At the other end of the scale, hiring advocates and removing resisters have less positive impact and greater likelihood for negative side effects.

Without contacts between advocates and apathetics, acceptance of the change diffuses much more slowly—if at all—through the population. People take the experience of credible colleagues seriously. Their credibility and their experience allows them to serve as references for the change to others who are affected by it. Without contacts, we attempt to rely on mass exposure to spread the word—which is unlikely to succeed. Walking the talk is equally critical. The old saying goes, "Actions speak louder than words." Leaders who exemplify the change every opportunity they have—who build the new way of working into their daily practices—say volumes about how serious the company is about the change.

In contrast, removing resisters and hiring advocates are levers that should be used only with caution—and only when it is absolutely necessary. They both have a small short-term benefit of shifting the population mix a bit toward advocates. However, this short-term benefit can easily be overshadowed by the negative side effects described previously. It is easy to focus on the resisters and blame them for any problems. There are times when it is appropriate to remove a resister—especially if he or she is in an influential position (see page 131). Similarly, there are times when the need for outside expertise is great enough to require hiring advocates. However, in most cases the side effects of these levers tend to outweigh their positive benefit in the long run—especially if they are used without very strong environmental support.

Apply the Goldilocks Test to the Levers of Change

Goldilocks sought out the porridge that was not too hot and not too cold and the chair that was not too big and not too small. The Goldilocks test is finding just the right level and not under- or over-using a lever. Clearly there are many Goldilocks tests that are driven by budget and resource constraints and balancing the many needs of a company, including implementing a change. However, there are innate specific Goldilocks constraints with respect to three levers—contacts, mass exposure, and reward and recognition—that deserve closer attention. They are all important levers, and they all have a role to play, but too much of a good thing can be detrimental.

For example, contacts are essential—they are how we leverage exponential growth (see the Power of Two on page 78). At the same time, you never want to burn out the advocates or put them in such a position that they are always advocating to the same people or neglecting real work. The last one is especially dangerous. If advocates are seen as doing nothing but advocating for a change, then their credibility as an advocate is *seriously* diminished. Similarly, some mass exposure is often necessary, but too much will backfire, especially if it is not fully supported by the environmental-support levers. (See shifting the burden on page 128). It is essential to match the mass exposure to the need for informing people on the change and no more. It is even more important to avoid hype; make no claims for a change that are not true.

Reward and recognition is another lever for which the Goldilocks test is useful—and surprisingly overlooked. A substantial portion of reward and recognition must be reserved for implementing the change. However, too much becomes confusing or even threatening. No company is in business just to make organizational changes, so the bulk of reward and recognition must be reserved for the product or service that the company is in business to provide. Applying the Goldilocks test to levers of change prevents wasted energy and expense that can become counterproductive.

There is no formula that can be universally applied for how much is just right. The level at which any of these levers becomes too much will vary with each organization and each change, but keeping Goldilocks in mind keeps us from going overboard when we have the resources or ignoring a lever when budget or other constraints are very tight.

Completing the Picture

To complete the picture of the Tipping Point model, we add these four sets of interactions to the model diagram. This gives the final diagram, shown below. You can see that the interactions and feedback loops are really what inform the model. It is a far cry from the image of independent variables each having an independent effect on the outcome from page 142.

A Fuller Picture of the Tipping Point Interactions

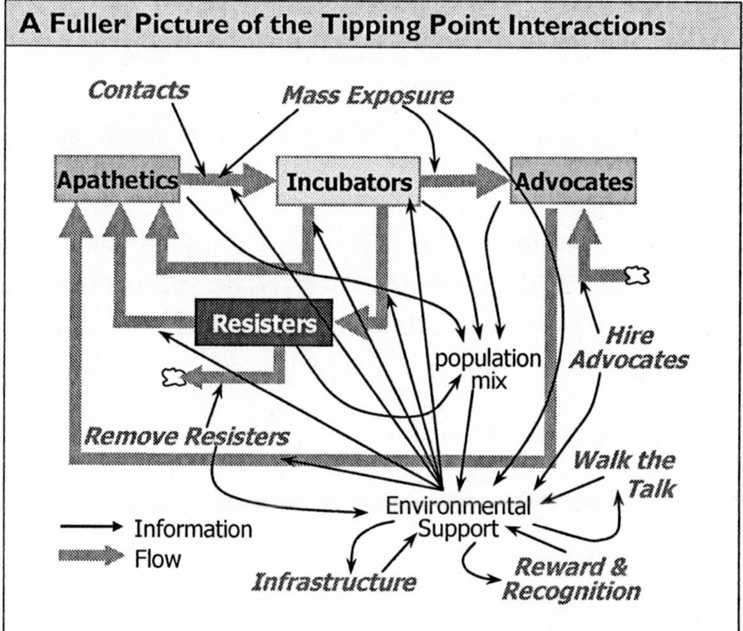

The dynamics described in this chapter have been added to the diagram from page 109 to give a fuller picture of the interactions inherent in organizational change. The Tipping Point model takes these interactions and feedback loops into account.

It is difficult to hold all the interactions and their consequences in mind. At least, it would be difficult for me to hold them all in my mind at once. Thus, you can see the value of a simulation; it allows you to experience the interactions—especially in a workshop setting where you can discuss the results and how they apply in your organization. The following chapter goes into detail on the using the simulation.

Moving Forward

Key Concepts

- There is no silver bullet. No single action that leaders can take guarantees successful change. Understanding how to put the seven levers into practice in your organization and how they interact is key to successful implementation.

- Some mass exposure is necessary, but it is probably the most overworked lever of change. Worse yet, overusing it typically has serious side effects that hinder acceptance of the change.

- Remember the four categories of interactions among the levers of change: (1) What goes around, comes around. (2) Combinations matter. (3) Not all levers of change are equal. (4) Apply the Goldilocks test to any lever of change.

Points to Ponder

- Are you constantly thinking about possible side effects, both short-term and long-term, from actions taken to implement change without letting "analysis paralysis" slow your progress?

- Do you have a mechanism in place to monitor unexpected negative side effects? What about unexpected successes?
- Do you feel confident that all the key players are "on the same page"? Do they share a common mental model of the goal and how to get there?

Chapter 6

Applying the Tipping Point

The concepts behind the Tipping Point model can be applied to any significant organizational change. Using the computer simulation in a workshop setting makes it easier. It brings the ideas in the model alive and fosters productive conversation. This chapter begins by outlining what you can expect from the simulation and ends with a case study from a large telecommunications company. The case study demonstrates how the Tipping Point workshop provides an environment for a team to think out of the box and create an improved, more effective implementation strategy.

Getting Results from the Simulation

It's what you learn after you know it all that counts.
— John Wooden

An intellectual understanding of the dynamics of change is important. Even more important is experiencing them. Because the Tipping Point model is captured in a compelling simulation, it can be used in a workshop setting to help managers experience the dynamics and interacting factors that affect the spread of organizational change. As with most management simulators, its value is not in its predictive power but in its ability to catalyze reflective conversation and foster understanding. Too often people responsible for implementing an organizational change rely on familiar techniques, such as poster campaigns and mass training, despite limited success with these methods in the past. Getting these people together to play with the simulation in an open atmosphere creates an experiential and experimental learning environment. It helps teams improve their implementation strategies, and it is also fun.

A simulation can accelerate the learning cycle from a change effort, which is normally slow and often costly. From the start of a change effort to the end is typically a fair amount of time; it could be a couple of years or more. At the end we have more information about change. If we are lucky, we've done some kind of formal lessons learned or had some group dialogue. This increases the information that we have about this change effort, which in turn increases our general knowledge of organizational change management. We can apply this knowledge the next time around, but this is just not good enough. We have to learn faster.

A computer simulation that sparks dialogue also accelerates learning. We apply what we know about change to the simulation and see and talk about the results immediately. This dialogue increases our overall knowledge of organizational change and helps us think as a team. All of this further adds to our knowledge about organizational change management in a way that we can apply right now—when it counts—not just to the next change effort. Accelerated learning using simulations was explored in a master's thesis by Osamu Yamamura. The following diagram is adapted from his work.

Increase Ability to Learn Quickly and as a Team

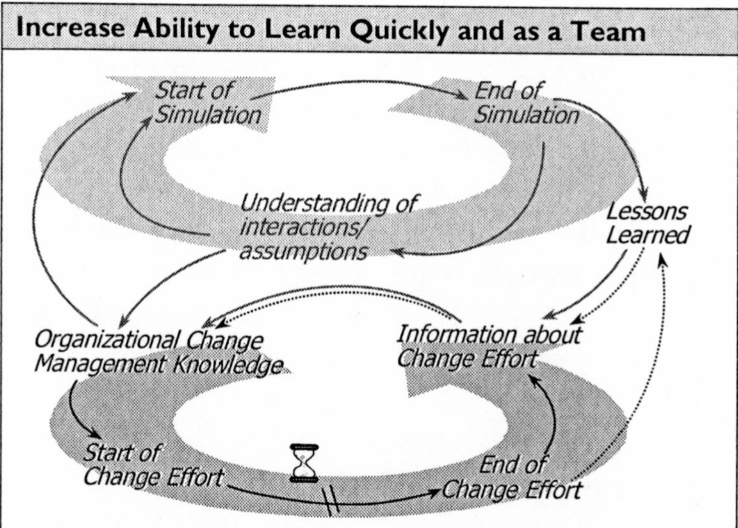

The simulation adds a low-risk, cost-effective engine of learning that leverages the knowledge of the team; it accelerates the learning cycle, which is typically slow and costly.

The lower loop (darker arrow) represents our learning cycle from a change effort. It takes time to implement a change and get information from it. What we learn from this change effort increases our overall knowledge about change, which we can apply to the next change effort. *If* we do a formal lessons learned (represented by the dotted line), it further adds to our information about the change effort. This increases our overall knowledge about change management—but it is still too late to apply it to the current change initiative.

The upper loop (lighter arrow) represents using a simulation such as the Tipping Point in a workshop setting. The workshop is structured to foster dialogue, learn from each other, and bring out lessons learned immediately. This increases our knowledge of change management. More important, we can apply these lessons right away—to the current organizational change initiative that we are facing.

It is important to be clear about what to expect from the Tipping Point simulation. It is not an answer machine. It is a powerful tool that can focus dialogue on change implementation. Using the simulation in a friendly, competitive environment helps teams see each other's assumptions about change. As people play the game, they get new ideas, they experiment, and they see interactions that they had not considered before. Through this process, they learn from each other. They get a richer picture—a richer mental model—of the task at hand.

The Tipping Point Workshop

> Learning is discovering that something is possible.
> — Fritz Perls

Getting people who are responsible for implementing a change together to play with the simulation in a friendly atmosphere creates a learning environment. A simulation helps us ask what-if questions. It broadens our perspective by providing a venue to step back and get a bird's eye view as we see the effect of the interactions unfold over time. Using a simulation with team members provides the opportunity to reflect on the organization as the team knows it and create shared mental models of challenges that they are facing. This dialogue and reflection is key to creating successful implementation plans that make organizational change both contagious and sustainable.

Participating in a Tipping Point workshop demonstrates that the simulation works to focus dialogue and create a shared mental model of change implementation. There is also objective evidence; Michelle Shields investigated the Tipping Point's ability to stimulate learning as part of her dissertation work. Her investigation used experimental field research, which she conducted at a major airline.

Her goal was to measure both learning and team involvement using a case study versus using the Tipping Point simulation. On tasks designed to measure understanding of complexity, she found that the groups using the simulation did better. More important, she asked participants in her experiment if they felt that the team strategy reflected their personal input. She found that individuals who were in teams that used the simulation felt that they had more input to the final team strategy than did individuals in teams who used the case study. That is, using the Tipping Point help move the team toward a shared mental model of what is required to create change. A shared mental model goes a long way to creating the type of buy-in necessary to successfully implement a change strategy.

The Tipping Point's ability to create a shared mental model is illustrated by a firm that used it when implementing a more market focused process for product development.

Create a Shared Mental Model using the Tipping Point

A high-tech firm found itself in a position where product decisions were made according to technical feasibility rather than market needs. As a result they were introducing some products for which there was little demand. To help them become more responsive to customers' expectations and to reduce their development costs, they introduced a product development process. The new process was designed to make product decisions based on market demands, to decrease the product development interval, and create value for the customer.

The implementation team used the Tipping Point workshop to help them focus their discussions around their project plans. As a result of discussing simulation results they gained a very rich understanding of both the interactions captured by the simulation and each other's ideas about change implementation. They realized as a team that they were relying too heavily on passive elements, especially mass exposure. They modified their plan to make key stakeholders accountable for active engagement around the elements of the new process. Years after implementing the new process, they report how the simulation helped them "sing off the same song sheet" and improve their implementation plan.

Tipping Point Workshop Structure

The experiential structure of a Tipping Point workshop is unique relative to most computer simulation workshops. Others are centered on people experimenting directly with the simulation. This typically results in "gaming behavior" where people just attempt to beat the computer. The Tipping Point workshop compels people to discuss, formulate, and document a strategy. Only after they have documented their strategy and the logic behind it can they try it on the simulation. This encourages team interaction and dialogue and prevents people just trying strategies without thinking about what they represent.

The Tipping Point workshop flow reinforces learning and facilitates planning. Initially the model is introduced with a series of real-world examples to reinforce the concepts. Then teams compete with each other to create strategies to apply to the simulated organization. This competition reinforces the model concepts and it sparks dialogue to help team members understand each other's assumptions about change implementation. Through the competition and the dialogue, team members form a shared mental model of change. This common mental model is richer and more complete than the models held by any of the individual members of the team. Finally, the workshop provides a structure to apply the learning to a change initiative facing the organization—making real progress.

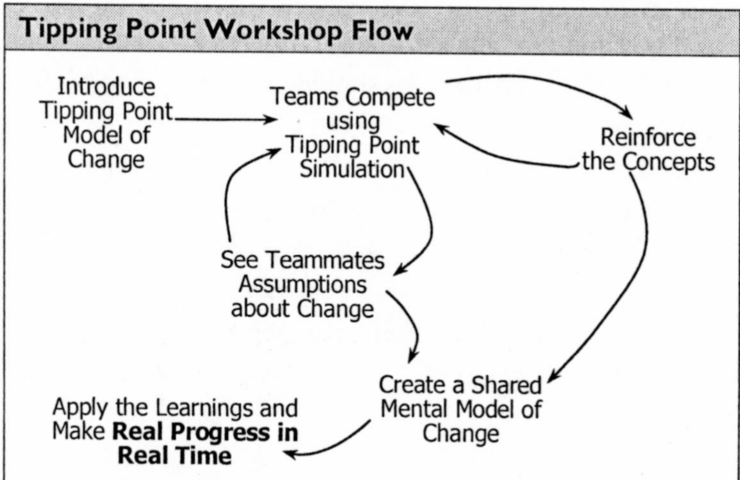

Too often people responsible for implementing an organizational change rely on familiar techniques—such as poster campaigns and mass training—despite experiencing limited success with these methods in the past. Getting these people together to play with the simulation in a workshop atmosphere can break this cycle.

The format of a Tipping Point workshop is interactive, experiential, and experimental. The flow begins by explaining the basics of the simulation and the theory behind it. The emphasis here is on the variables and what they mean. Next, participants break into teams. The teams will use the strategy sheet in their workbooks to define their strategy for implementing change. Competition between teams reinforces the new theory represented by the Tipping Point model and provides an opportunity to voice assumptions and to listen to others. Together the new model of change and a better view of each other's assumptions helps give teams a shared mental model of implementing change. Finally, participants apply the learnings. They briefly glance backward to see how the Tipping Point could have improved a previous change implementation. Then, they brainstorm about the new concerns and opportunities with the current change that have been brought out by the workshop. Last, they create action items from the concerns and opportunities.

The Tipping Point workshop is effective because it gets people involved. It's fun; the simulation is engaging to play with. The competition built into the workshop adds a dimension that increases people's involvement. While devising strategies to beat the other teams, participants discuss their ideas and hidden assumptions about organizational change. Once people are involved and thinking about change strategies, they can have a more serious discussion on organizational change. This helps teams form strategies that are richer and understood fully by everyone.

Using the Simulation: A Case Study[x]

> The best parachute folders are those who jump.
> — Anonymous

Transforming a large, successful organization with facilities around the world to meet the needs of a changing market is a challenging undertaking. Nortel Networks' executive team concluded that to remain successful, the company needed to integrate its product lines more closely. It was not sufficient for products to work together technically. Nortel needed to manage orders and order delivery across lines of business to present a single face to the customer. They realized that to make an overhaul of this magnitude they needed improved processes that spanned product lines, new technology, and the support of their people. Not surprisingly, the people part of this triad proved to be the most crucial. Everything else hinged on employees' willingness and ability to implement the new processes and use the new technology.

Nortel is a leading data and telecommunications supplier and manufacturer, with thousands of employees worldwide and markets on all continents. At the time of this undertaking, the company consisted of five lines of business (LOBs)—separately serving the needs of data, voice, public, private, and wireless networks—each with its own products, processes, and delivery mechanisms. For example, the individual LOBs had order management and order delivery systems that worked well for them. However, independent systems for each LOB were not conducive to supplying customers with networks that integrated products from multiple LOBs. At the time, a minority of customers ordered integrated networks. However, Nortel anticipated that the market was shifting and the need to integrate products from across several LOBs would be a significant factor in the future. Nortel launched a Supply Chain Management (SCM) program to address its customers' future needs for integrated network solutions. The goal of the initiative was to present customers with a single interface that would make it easier for them to order products for integrated voice and data networks from across the LOBs.

The SCM executive sponsor and his team created a vision of how the supply chain would function to meet customer needs into the future. He put together teams to implement the new processes and technology. To deal with the people aspect of SCM, he assigned a three-person management team to oversee the organizational change management, training, and communication efforts around the vision. This team then recruited people from the 28 Nortel locations worldwide to serve as ambassadors of change. Ambassadors were members of their local SCM implementation teams with training or communications responsibilities for their sites. Initially, there were 37 ambassadors.

The ambassadors' mission was to engage employees in adapting and adopting the SCM vision as their own. They sought more than simple buy-in by local units; they wanted to cultivate a real sense of ownership among fellow employees for the new systems and recognition that SCM was the right thing to do. The ambassadors soon faced their first challenge: People within each LOB saw their own processes as working well—in fact, they were working well when taken from the viewpoint of each individual LOB. Without a sense that anything was broken, many people found it difficult to accept the need for change and the need to take a broader view of their role in the system as a whole. At first, the ambassadors did not have the tools to overcome this resistance, but that soon changed.

Nortel sponsored a Change Leaders' Conference. The event offered those involved in training, organizational development, employee communication, and various change initiatives throughout the company a chance to learn from each other's successes. Among the 80 participants at the conference were 20 or more of the ambassadors, along with the three-person corporate leadership team. The program included hands-on experience with the Tipping Point simulation. At the conference, several teams vied with each other to design the best strategy for increasing the number of simulated advocates of a change initiative while keeping the simulated costs down. The charged atmosphere of the friendly competition catalyzed conversation about organizational change and gave people an opportunity to experiment with their ideas. Many participants left the session with insights about implementing change—both from the innovative model and from the dialogue with their team members, which was sparked by the friendly competition.

For the ambassadors, concepts from the Tipping Point not only helped create a common language around change but also became the building blocks for the people and organizational portion of the overall SCM implementation. The ideas that were most influential were: (1) the concept that advocates are people who accept and apply a change, (2) the importance of connections between advocates and others, and (3) the role that upper management plays by modeling desired behaviors. For example, the ambassadors used the language from the Tipping Point in their weekly planning sessions. They talked about spreading the word. They identified key advocates and set clear goals around the number of contacts they wanted to foster between advocates and those not yet infected at each location. The ambassadors created situations for advocates to meet with people who needed to hear about the new ideas. This process set the stage for the implementation that followed. They coached the leadership in what was required to walk the talk and the message that it sent if they failed to do so.

The three-person management team also used the simulation with top management. For the SCM executive sponsor, this experience reinforced the value of using a common language to discuss SCM implementation and the informal manner in which ideas spread throughout an organization. He identified ways he could help foster commitment by walking the talk and by taking advantage of the power of his position; for example, by ensuring that he himself sent personal thank-you notes for jobs well done during the transition.

The ambassadors encountered some resistance to their approach. In one case, an ambassador felt that she was not getting through to the leader of her implementation team. The group was planning to embark on a traditional rollout, which consisted mostly of printed material, mass emails, and some general awareness training. Their plan did not consider the notion that ideas can be contagious at all. It did not foster contacts between advocates and others; it did not even attempt to identify advocates within their organization. The ambassador appealed to the three-person corporate leadership team for assistance. Together they presented the Tipping Point simulation to the implementation team. The participants became quite involved with the game and engaged in heated debate about their simulated strategies. Days later, the implementation team changed its approach to communicating with the workforce about the SCM implementation to be more consistent with the strategy designed by the ambassadors. The simulation is not didactic; it does not provide answers on a silver platter. Rather it worked to focus the team. Team members themselves learned which approaches might be most effective for SCM implementation by talking through their simulated strategy. While playing the game, they learned from each other.

In the early stages of the SCM implementation, some locations experienced technology difficulties. The ambassadors' commitment was instrumental in bolstering morale and keeping people focused on the goal. The ambassadors from those early applications documented valuable lessons learned, including both successes and pitfalls to avoid. They passed these lessons on to sites implementing SCM later in the cycle. The network of contacts between the advocates who had experience with SCM and those who did not, which had been fostered by the ambassadors, helped smooth the implementation at the later sites. These contacts helped put difficulties into perspective and helped lessons learned reach areas where they could be applied most effectively.

At Nortel, creating the ambassadors of change was an important first step in shifting from an emphasis on optimizing local processes to a systemic view of the company as a whole. The Tipping Point simulation provided a platform for real learning about change. It gave the ambassadors a common language for talking about organizational change and an opportunity to experience the value of creating connections to foster change. It helped focus the ambassadors' strategy. It gave them a novel way to look at change from a people perspective. It gave them insights into how the people affected actually make the internal changes that result in organizational change. They developed effective ways to foster contagious commitment among employees—giving them a smoother road to implementation.

Preparing for Change

Experience is the name everyone gives to their mistakes.
— Oscar Wilde

In organizations, managers are rewarded for action. Sometimes this leads to shooting from the hip with almost predictable side effects. Often it is imperative to take a step back and reevaluate our position before jumping to action. A checklist can be a useful tool to help us step back. Nonetheless, I offer this checklist with some hesitation. A checklist gives a very linear impression. It also makes all elements of the list appear equal. Never use the checklist alone—spend a few minutes reviewing the dynamics and the interactions inherent in change that are captured in the Tipping Point model before using the checklist. Once you have used the Tipping Point in a workshop, the following checklist can help in assessing how well the organization is using the levers of change and what areas need emphasis in your organization's change strategy.

A Checklist for Change
Contacts between Advocates and Apathetics •Are the advocates identified? •Are the advocates respected for their expertise in the product or service that the company produces? •Can they apply the three skills described in the advocate skill section (on page 59)? •Can you foster contacts through town hall meetings or informal networks? •Are advocates being supported in implementing the change?
Mass Exposure •Does the mass exposure match the need? •Is the mass exposure always honest? Will it pass a no-hype test? •Is the mass exposure matched to the support for and commitment to the change? •What might we be doing too much of—or too little of?
Hire Advocates •Is there a way to leverage hiring to include new advocates when hiring for skill or growth? •Are you in danger of relying too much on hiring new advocates? •Are you monitoring the resentment that often results from hiring advocates?

A Checklist for Change

Remove Resisters

- Are we listening to the concerns of resisters and making adjustments as appropriate?
- Are pockets of resistance identified?
- Do we have a plan to deal with resisters?
- Is there resistance in key places?
- Are we confusing apathy with resistance?

Reward and Recognition

- Are reward and recognition plans in place?
- Are we looking for the behaviors that make the change work and rewarding the business results from those behaviors?
- Are we leveraging recognition—including informal recognition?
- Is there a plan in place to reward or recognize early wins?

Infrastructure

- Does the schedule match the work to be done? Do stakeholders understand the schedule?
- Do people understand how they will do their jobs once the change is implemented?
- Is there a plan for job specific training in place?
- Are the tools, technology, data, and infrastructure in place?
- Is there harmful infrastructure (e.g., policies) that must be removed?
- Are there tools in place to measure progress?

A Checklist for Change

Walk the Talk

- Is it clear who the sponsor is?
- Does everyone involved understand the vision and the success criteria?
- Is leadership making the business need/opportunity clear, and do all stakeholders recognize it?
- Are the decision makers and the decision-making process visible to those affected?
- Does every stakeholder see the link between company performance, the change initiative, and their own performance?
- Are all the company systems (i.e., compensation, operational reviews, business strategy) aligned with the change?

Interactions

- What areas need to be addressed simultaneously? Sequentially?
- What areas might undermine others? Enhance others?
- What other areas provide opportunities or concerns?
- What actions in your culture can make an idea contagious?

When you are designing your implementation plan, think first about your advocates. What can you do to support them? Use the checklist with three things in mind. How do I use the levers of change to (1) get new advocates, (2) keep the advocates that I already have, and (3) increase the capacity of the advocates to spread the change? Remember that the levers are not equal, and they will interact to increase or possibly interfere with each other's effectiveness. Revisit the checklist from time to time to assess progress or modify plans as you implement your change.

Moving Forward

Key Concepts

- Simulations are a low-risk, cost-effective way to accelerate learning—especially learning as a team. Simulations should never be used as answer machines. Every organization and every change is different. A simulation is a way to bring out interactions and feedback loops that might otherwise be missed.

- The Tipping Point simulation—especially used in a workshop—has a proven ability to help teams focus their dialogue on implementing an organizational change.

- Use the checklist to mitigate shooting from the hip, but always keep the interactions in mind.

Points to Ponder

- Do you have a tool or process that encourages people to think out of the box with this change?

- Does everyone involved in this change understand all the factors and how they interact to create change?

Conclusion

It is easier to attain leadership than to maintain it.
— Alfred P. Sloan

We do business in a world of change—change that is driven by political, economic, social, and technical (PEST) factors that are constantly in flux. Organizations must be able to make internal organizational changes to adapt to and take advantage of the PEST. Each of us has been through many organizational change initiatives, and we have the logo coffee mugs to prove it. Unfortunately, most of these organizational change initiatives fail. The time is ripe for a new model of organizational change—a fresh way to think about how change happens in organizations. The Tipping Point model can provide this new view of change.

We know that ideas can be contagious. When ideas are about new and better ways of working, we want to make them contagious. Lessons from public health, systems thinking, and organizational theory provide the key to making ideas contagious. The Tipping Point model puts them together and creates a map to make a needed organizational change both contagious and sustainable. This combination of lessons learned from public health, thinking systemically, and proven organizational theory creates a powerful tool for change.

The Tipping Point model is useful only if it improves results. In organizational change, results mean producing a successful implementation. The Tipping Point model helps improve results in two ways. First, it highlights important and relevant issues that are missed in less systemic models of change. By doing so, it improves chances of finding areas of leverage in change implementation plans. Second, it is a significant communication tool. It provides teams with a powerful common language to discuss and plan the change process. This common language helps them communicate about the implementation and create a shared view of what it takes to succeed. It helps them align their expectations, and recognize—as a team—when they are on course.

The Tipping Point is a dynamic model of change. The dynamics of the Tipping Point model result from recognizing that people's attitude toward a change initiative can and does change over time. The Tipping Point takes into account four attitudes that people may have toward a change initiative: (1) advocates—people with experience, expertise, and enthusiasm toward the change; (2) incubators—people who are trying to understand its effects; (3) apathetics—people who feel disconnected from the change; and (4) resisters—people who are opposing or pushing back against the change. Leaders can have an effect on how a change spreads by using seven levers of change: (1) contacts between advocates and apathetics, (2) the level of mass exposure, (3) hiring new advocates, (4) addressing resistance, (5) rewards and recognition, (6) investing in infrastructure, such as equipment or other support, and (7) leaders who walk the talk. Levers 1–4 directly affect the advocate-apathetic mix and are people-support levers. Levers 5–7 are called environmental-support levers because they influence the context for the change. The right combination of advocacy and support can help ensure timely change implementation.

Because the Tipping Point model has been implemented in a computer simulation, it enables management to gain "flight simulator" experience with it. Used in a workshop setting, the simulation can help team members bring to the surface and challenge their own assumptions and beliefs that produce actions and decisions around implementing organizational change. The simulation allows us to surface those assumptions in a low-risk environment, before risking business results by applying them to our change strategy.

Creating a competitive workshop environment in which teams try to outwit each other with a faster and cheaper strategy in a safe, simulated environment generates enthusiasm and thereby learning. The strongest learning feature is not from the outputs of the simulation—rather, it is from creating an open dialogue between team members. Playing in a simulated environment leads to experimentation and discussion that broadens understanding. Because it also compresses time, we can see the effect of the interactions play out in a few seconds rather than several months or years. Further, we can discuss those effects. We can trace them back to the structure of the model, which we can map onto our understanding of change. The simulation in the competitive atmosphere provides focus for learning. It helps people articulate their own mental models, so that teams create a shared mental model of implementing change.

The workshop leverages the computer simulation to create dialogue and teamwork, which results in a shared view of change. This shared view is really the first step in making a change sustainable. Challenging assumptions and leveraging knowledge leads to deeper insight and more effective actions and helps create a culture of learning. Creating a culture of learning—learning quickly and as a team—can be a tipping point toward extraordinary business results.

The most important organizational change is useless unless it can be implemented. Depending on which researcher you read 50–85% of all organizational change initiatives fail. This means that many needed, well-analyzed, and technically suitable changes never provide business value. They fail due to ignorance of how the change process works in organizations. Thus, it is as important for an organizational change to be implementable as it is for it to be appropriate. When leaders implement, or attempt to implement, a needed organizational change, they make a number of choices. With this book—and the Tipping Point model—they can make good choices, adept choices, choices that lead to effective deployment strategies.

The Tipping Point model of change provides the framework to improve the choices leaders make when designing change implementation strategies. The Tipping Point model of change is built on the concept that commitment to an organizational change spreads when people understand its value to their own jobs; these people demonstrate and advocate the change to others in the organization. If people are committed to a change they will work to achieve it. Leadership must foster the environment that increases commitment and thereby the number of advocates supporting a change.

Leaders are responsible for finding and instigating those actions that perturb the organization away from the status quo and toward the changes that can have significant effect. There is no panacea; every organization is different. A systemic model like the Tipping Point makes the framework available to think through effective ways to perturb the system and create change.

We all know that reality is more complex than any model. But the distilled environment created by a simulation is an effective starting point to test the ideas and foster the dialogues that are prerequisite for successful change.

Appendix 1: More on Models of Change

Kurt Lewin

Many models of change, in fact many modern social theories, have their roots in the early work of Kurt Lewin. His model of change is often called unfreezing, moving, and refreezing. In his view, an organization is constantly under the effect of opposing forces, forces of change and forces of the status quo. When these forces are roughly equal, the organization is in what Lewin terms a "quasi-stationary equilibrium." In his view, change is best accomplished by reducing the forces of the status quo, which he calls unfreezing the organization. He suggests "psychological disconfirmation" to facilitate unfreezing, which is accomplished by making the case for the change very clear. To create successful change, all stakeholders must understand the challenges driving it, why the current position of the organization is inadequate, and the consequences of not making the change. The next step, moving, involved establishing the new behaviors and attitudes needed for its new challenges. The final step is refreezing, which is focused on establishing the necessary infrastructure to support the new status quo.

Kurt Lewin Saw Change as a Process

In Lewin's view, change was a three-step process. (1) Unfreezing—clearly establishing the case for change as well an understanding that the current situation was inadequate. (2) Moving—establishing the norms and behaviors necessary to make the change successful. (3) Refreezing—establishing the infrastructure to do business in the changed environment.

Marvin Weisbord

Marvin Weisbord's six-box model provides a way to understand an organization and thereby how change can happen within it. The six boxes in his model are (1) purpose or clarity about the goals of the organization; (2) structure or the infrastructure in place to achieve the goals; (3) relationships, which include relationships between departments and between people; (4) rewards, which include all incentives and punishments; (5) helpful mechanisms or the basic processes that any company must have to survive; and (6) leadership, which has the special role of monitoring all the boxes and maintaining the big picture of how they interact. In Weisbord's view, diagnosing these six interacting areas, visually represented as boxes, explains how the organization exists in its environment. He says that there are formal and informal systems at work in each of the boxes, the formal prescribes how work should get done and the informal describes how work really does get done. Any successful change agent must monitor the effects of the change on all of the boxes and their interactions, both formal and informal.

Marvin Weisbord's Six-Box Model
In Weisbord's model, six aspects of the organization interact via both formal and informal mechanisms. Leadership has the central role of coordinating the actions of the other five boxes, which are Purpose, Relationships, Helpful Mechanisms, Rewards, and Structure. Thus, Leadership is central to how organizations work and how effective change initiatives can be.

William Bridges

William Bridges's transitions model is concerned with how change affects individuals. It examines the psychological transitions that people go through when they are exposed to change and the pattern that these transitions follow. Because organizations change when people in them change, it is important to understand the pattern of psychological changes within individuals undergoing an organizational change. According to Bridges, there are three phases people go through as part of a significant change. The phases are (1) letting go or ending phase, in which people need time to grapple with losing something that has become familiar and safe; (2) neutral zone, during which people need time to comprehend what the new order will be like once the change is implemented and how they can fit into it and be productive; and (3) new beginning, where people begin to behave in the new ways that are required by the change. Bridges claims that one of the biggest challenges of leading change occurs because the leader knows about the change long before others in the organization. Therefore, he or she has spent time in the first two phases, at least, before the change is announced to most employees. Forgetting that they themselves took time to go through the phases, leaders see employees who are just beginning the letting go phase as rigid or even hostile to the change.

Bridges Recognizes that People go through Transitional Stages before Accepting a Change

According to Bridges, at any point in time people who are higher in management have had more time to learn about and deal with a change—so they are farther along on the psychological transitions path. Because it is hard for them to remember how it felt to be in a previous stage, they see people in the earlier stages as hostile to the change when they are actually just in the earlier stages of processing it and its effect on themselves.

John Kotter

John Kotter emphasizes the role of leadership in creating important organizational change. He asserts that 85% of companies that he has studied fail to make needed transformations because managers do not recognize their roles in leading change. He recommends eight steps that leaders must follow to improve their success rate. In the eight steps, Kotter outlines the leader's responsibility to explain the need for the change, what the end state will look like, and who will guide the day-to-day efforts. He recognizes that the people affected by the change must be empowered, and the leader's role is to remove obstacles. Kotter emphasizes the importance of early successes in creating change. The leader must create the environment for those early wins, make sure that everyone hears about them, and use them to institutionalize the change. He reminds us that there are leaders at every level of the organization, people with a desire to learn and a willingness to take risks. People look to their leadership. Effective leaders lead by example. In Kotter's view behavior that is inconsistent with the vision of the change will "overwhelm other forms of communication."

Kotter Emphasizes Leadership's Role in Change
Kotter outlines eight steps that leaders must take to create successful change.
1. *Establish a Sense of Urgency*—Based on market and competitive realities, identify the problems of continuing with the status quo and the opportunities available from the change. 2. *Form a Powerful Guiding Coalition*—Form a team that works together and has enough power to guide the change effort and is committed to its success. 3. *Create a Vision*—Create a clear, well-articulated picture of where the organization is headed and strategies for getting

there.

4. *Communicate the Vision*—Use every means available to communicate the vision and strategy, especially via the behaviors of the guiding coalition.
5. *Empower Others to Act on the Vision*—Look for obstacles to change, such as processes or structures, and remove them. Encourage risk taking.
6. *Plan for and Create Short-Term Wins*—Create credibility for the change by planning and demonstrating improvements. Recognize and reward employees involved in early wins.
7. *Consolidate Gains and Produce More Change*—Use the credibility from initial short-term wins to further the systems, processes, structures, policies, or employees who embody the vision.
8. *Institutionalize the New Approaches*—Draw out the connections between the change and the organization's success. Anchor the change in the corporate culture using rewards and succession.

Daryl Conner

Daryl Conner describes many of the important factors driving change implementation in organizations. Two aspects of his theory are important here. The first is the notion of participatory management, which means that all stakeholders' voices are heard. Sometimes we confuse participatory management with copping out or with evading responsibilities as managers. This is far from Conner's idea. Rather, he recognizes that people are more likely to support a change when their opinions have been heard and addressed whenever possible. A second important aspect of Conner's change theory is the roles that people play in implementing change. In his view, there are four important roles involved in change implementation. (1) Sponsors have the leadership role and identify the change that is needed and have the authority to mandate it. (2) Agents are responsible for planning and implementing the change. (3) Targets are the focus of the change effort. They are expected to make the change—to use the new process or new technology. (4) Advocates believe the value and goals of the change but lack the authority to sanction it. According to Conner, if there is no reporting relationship between the targets and the agents, then change initiatives usually fail. The archetypal example of this lack of reporting structure is targets who are line managers, but change agents who are in HR or another support function.

Conner's Four Roles in Implementing Change
Conner outlines "role axioms" for the four roles he describes.
Sponsors—Avoid overcommitment. Without sufficient sponsorship initiatives fail, costing the company and tarnishing the sponsor.
Agents—Avoid "bad business," when the sponsor has not sanctioned the change to the targets or lacks the resolve to see the change through. Never try to take on the role of the sponsor or attempt to compensate for inadequate sponsorship.
Targets—Seek clarity. Don't participate in a change unless you are clear what is expected of you or how committed the sponsor is.
Advocates—Don't confuse your enthusiasm for the change with proper sponsorship.

Appendix 2: Notation of Links and Loops

The language of links and loops is the language of systems thinking. With this language we can understand the structure of a system, and this structure drives the events and behaviors that we experience. An apocryphal story about a city family that moved to the country to farm helps illustrate just how structure drives behavior. A local farmer stops in to visit and finds a scene of great confusion. The cow's head is stuck between the boards of the fence. All the members of the city family are trying to shove her head back. The cow is bawling, and the kids are screaming. The local farmer picks up the bucket of oats from outside the pen and puts it inside the pen. The cow immediately twists her head and frees it from between the boards of the fence and munches the oats.

The language of links and loops is simple and straightforward and can describe the structure of any system. First, consider the links. Simple arrows represent two components that are linked in a causal relationship—so an arrow from A to B indicates that A causes or drives B. The arrows are labeled, with either an s for same or an o for opposite. So an arrow from A to B labeled with an s means that they move in the same direction; when A goes up, then B goes up and when A goes down, then B goes down. An o means they move in the opposite direction—when A goes up, then B goes down, and when A goes down, then B goes up. The last notation is a cross-hatch with an hourglass used to indicate a link where a delay is a serious consideration.

Tokens Used to Label Links	
The arrows in link-and-loop diagrams represent causal relationships. In both of the examples to the right A causes B. When A goes up, it can cause B to go up or down. An arrow labeled with an s indicates that when A goes up then B will go up—they move in the same direction. If the arrow is labeled with an o, then A and B move in opposite directions. So if A goes up then B goes down.	 B moves in the same direction as A. When A goes up, then B goes up. When A goes down, then B goes down.
	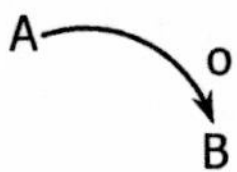 B moves in the opposite direction from A. When A goes up, then B goes down. When A goes down, then B goes up.
A link with a cross-hatch and an hourglass next to it indicates that time is a factor in that link. In particular it means that it takes time for A to have its effect on B.	 There is a time delay between A and B.

The interactions in systems that are represented by these links hook up to form closed loops, which are known as feedback loops. There are only two types of feedback loops—reinforcing and balancing. They form the basic building blocks of systems thinking. Each type of loop has it own characteristic dynamics. These dynamics combine with each other to create more complex patterns. Reinforcing loops drive the system away from a steady state, toward growth or decline. Balancing loops try to put the system into a steady state.

Reinforcing and balancing loops each have their own notation. Balancing loops are sometimes labeled with a seesaw icon (to indicate balance) or a negative sign in parentheses. Here we label them with a simple B in the center. A snowball going downhill (to represent building on itself) is often used to label a reinforcing loop as is a positive sign in parentheses. In this book, we will chose the simple R in the center of the loop. When a diagram has more than one balancing or reinforcing loop they are numbered B1, B2, and so on for balancing loops or R1, R2, and so on for reinforcing loops. An example of a simple balancing loop follows to put the notation together.

House Heating System Forms a Balancing Loop

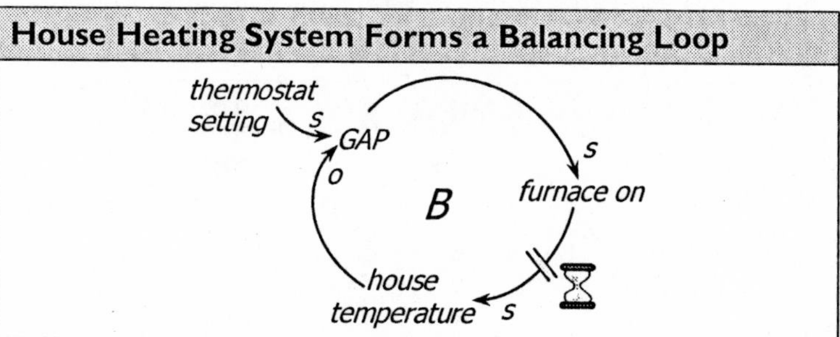

The way the heating system in your home works is an example of a balancing loop. Working in combination, the thermostat and the furnace keep the temperature in the house as close as possible to the goal temperature set on the thermostat. When the house temperature drops below the goal temperature, the thermostat senses it and turns on the furnace. This raises the house temperature, thereby lowering the gap between the thermostat setting and the house temperature. When the gap is zero (or very small in sophisticated thermostats), the thermostat turns off the furnace. If it is colder outside, the house will begin to cool down. When the temperature drops below the thermostat setting the process starts all over again

To finish the explanation of link and loop notation, let's examine a simple reinforcing loop: compound interest in a savings account. The annual change in the balance begins small, but if left to accrue interest it reaches a tipping point and the annual growth becomes suddenly very large, getting larger each year.

Imagine your great-great-great-great grandfather opened a savings account with £10 deposit at 2% interest before boarding the *Mayflower* for the New World in 1620. His account would be worth £192,870 in 2002. The same savings account would have been worth only £2,200 at the time of the American Revolution, £12,300 during the Civil War, and £63,000 after World War II. Relatively little interest accrued in the first 150 years, whereas well over half of it accrued in the last 50 years. In fact, banks understand the tipping point, which is why they do not pay interest on accounts left dormant for too many years.

Great-...-great Grandfather's Savings Account

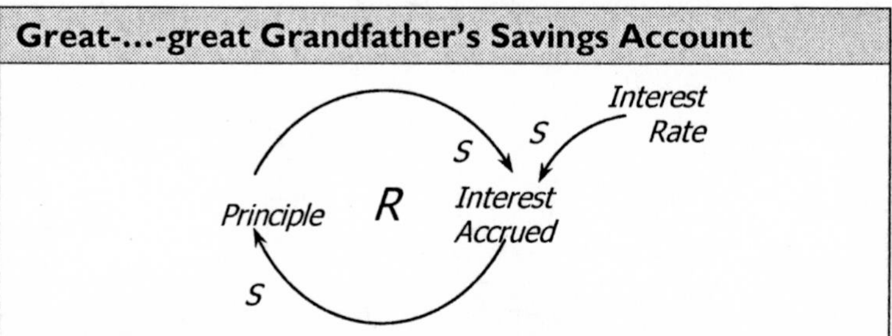

Compound interest is another example of exponential growth. As the principal goes up, the accrued interest goes up, which further drives up the principal.

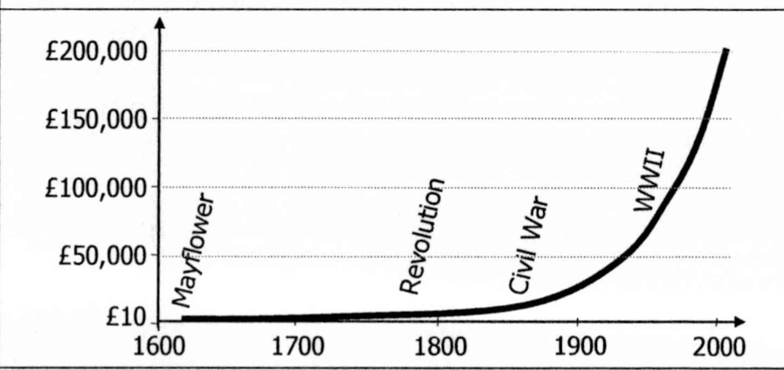

The diagram on the above shows the principal growth on a hypothetical savings account with £10 deposited at 2% interest for nearly 400 years shows the characteristic of slow growth before reaching a tipping point and rapid growth afterward. Now, if you could just find that passbook...

Endnotes

---

[i] See Yong and Wilkinson (TQM), Lancaster (BPR), Malbert, Soni and Venkataramanan (ERP), or Rigby, Reichheld and Schefter (CRM) in Suggested Readings and Resources on page 189.

[ii] The anecdotes are from personal experience and experiences of my colleagues and clients. They are adapted to illustrate points made in the book. A few are composites of experiences in different organizations. My thanks to the many people who shared their experiences with me.

[iii] See Appendix 1: More on Models of Change for more on each of the models.

[iv] This diagram describes part of the process of the flu spreading. It captures some of the movement between the three pools, well, incubating, and contagious. We know that there is more to the picture. (For example, with the flu, in time most contagious people will also return to the well pool, and a few may die.) This diagram mirrors many in the book. As we build up the concepts of the Tipping Point model, we increase the detail and completeness of the corresponding diagrams.

[v] See Strebel, Kotter, or Lancaster in Suggested Reading and Resources for estimates of percentages of organizational changes that fail.

[vi] Ross and Roberts use *advocacy* in a very general way. Don't confuse it with being an advocate of a change.

[vii] The equation for the number of grains of sand is $\sum_{i=0}^{63} 2^i$.

This story is based on a classic folk tale that appears in many cultures. In it, a selfish king (or raj or emperor) is indebted to a poor woodcutter (or an elephant bather or servant). The king wants to give the minimum reward to the woodcutter. Underestimating how much he would owe, the king agrees to the woodcutter's "humble" idea to determine his reward by filling a chessboard with rice by doubling the grains of rice with each square. Long before all the squares on the chessboard are filled, the king realizes that value of the rice needed to fill the board is so high that he owes his entire kingdom to the woodcutter, who also marries his daughter.

[viii] See Appendix 2: Notation of Links and Loops for more on the savings account example.

[ix] The tipping ratio = ratio of new advocates to former advocates = 100 new advocates / 100 former advocates = 1.0.

[x] This section is adapted from an article that I wrote with Carol Lorenz that appeared in the *System Thinker* in August 2000. Thanks to Nortel Networks for permission to use the case study.

Acknowledgements

Without the support and advice of many people this book would never have been possible. Let me first thank the clients and colleagues that I have worked with and learned from over the years. I also wish to thank Roger Bushnell, Kimm Hershberger, Art Kleiner, Rick Ross, Michelle Shields, Judy Seidenstein, Janet Smith, Sue Tideman and Carol Willett who read and commented on earlier drafts of the book. It has been strengthened by the extent that I heeded their comments, and any oversights are my own. Special thanks to Carol Lorenz who encouraged me to pursue System Dynamics Modeling and thus made the simulation a possibility. Sam Yamamura taught me the Japanese proverb that brilliantly illustrates the power of systems thinking. Conversations with George Smart helped me frame the position the book would occupy. I also owe a special debt to Pat Carstensen and Jennie Ratcliffe whose unflinching willingness to hear and hone my latest idea contributed greatly to the intellectual backbone of the book. Finally my editor, Laura Poole, made my prose readable and Susan Bilheimer guided me through the production process.

Suggested Reading and Resources

Ackoff, Russell L. *Ackoff's Best.* New York: John Wiley & Sons, 1999.

Bridges, William. *Managing Transitions: Making the Most of Change.* Cambridge, MA: Perseus Publishing, 1992.

Conner, Daryl R. *Managing at the Speed of Change.* New York: Vallard Books, 1991.

Gladwell, Malcolm. *The Tipping Point: How Little Things Can Make a Big Difference.* Boston: Little, Brown, 2000.

Hirschhorn, Larry. "Campaigning for Change." *Harvard Business Review,* July 2002.

Kelly, Kevin. *New Rules for the New Economy.* New York: Penguin Books, 1998.

Kim, Chan and Mauborgne, Renee. "Fair Process: Managing in the Knowledge Economy." *Harvard Business Review,* July–August 1997.

Kotter, John P. *Leading Change.* Boston: Harvard Business School Press, 1997.

Lancaster, Hal. "Reengineering Authors Reconsider Reengineering." *Wall Street Journal,* January 17, 1995.

Malbert, Vincent, Ashok Soni and M. A. Venkataramanan. "Enterprise Resource Planning: Common Myths versus Evolving Reality." *Business Horizons,* May–June 2001.

McGregor, Douglas. *The Human Side of Enterprise.* New York: McGraw-Hill, 1960.

Meyer, Chris. "Keeping Pace with the Accelerating Enterprise." *CIO Insight*, November 2002. www.cioinsight.com/article2/0,3959,675333,00.asp.

Meadows, Donella. "Dancing with Systems." *Systems Thinker*, March 2002. www.thesystemsthinker.com.

Moore, Geoffrey. *Crossing the Chasm.* New York: HarperBusiness, 1991.

Musselwhite, Chris. *Change Style Indicator.* Discovery Learning, 2001. Information online at www.discoverylearning.com.

Orlikowski, Wanda J. and J. Debra Hofman. "An Improvisational Model of Change Management: The Case of Groupware Technologies." *Sloan Management Review*, Winter 1997.

Rigby, Darrell K., Frederick F. Reichheld and Phil Schefter. "Avoid the Four Perils of CRM." *Harvard Business Review*, February 2002.

Rogers, Everett. *Diffusion of Innovation*, 4th ed. New York: Free Press, 1995.

Schelling, Thomas C. "Thermostats, Lemons, and Other Families of Models." In *Micromotives and Macrobehavior*, New York: Norton, 1978.

Senge, Peter, Richard Ross, Art Kleiner, Charlotte Roberts, Bryan Smith. *The Fifth Discipline Fieldbook: Strategies and Tools for Building a Learning Organization.* New York: Doubleday, 1994.

Shapiro, Andrea. *Applying the Tipping Point to Organizational Change: A Simulation.* Strategy Perspective, 1998. Information on line at www.4-perspective.com.

Shields, Michelle. "An Experimental Investigation Comparing the Effects of Case Study and Management Flight Simulator in a Group Setting." Proceedings of the International Conference of the Systems Dynamics Society, 2001.

Sterman, John D. "System Dynamics Modeling: Tools for Learning in a Complex World." *California Management Review*, Summer 2001.

Strebel, Paul. "Why Do Employees Resist Change?" *Harvard Business Review*, May–June 1996.

Weisbord, Marvin Ross. *Organizational Diagnosis: A Workbook of Theory and Practice*. Reading, MA: Addison-Wesley, 1978.

Wheatley, Margaret and Myron Kellner-Rogers. *A Simpler Way*. San Francisco: Berrett-Koehler Publishers, 1996.

Yamamura, Osamu. "Improving Quality of the Concurrent Software Development Management Using a System Dynamics Model." Master's Thesis, North Carolina State University, Raleigh, NC, 1996.

Yong, Josephine and Adrian Wilkinson. "Rethinking Total Quality Management." *Total Quality Management*, 12, 2, 2001, 247–258.

Index

For more information on a Tipping Point Workshop or on training and certification please visit:

http://www.4-perspective.com

Dr. Andrea Shapiro has worked with Fortune 500 companies for over twenty years. Her goal is to enable organizations to optimize their effectiveness through innovative learning methods and improved decision making. She brings a unique perspective to organizational change, which stems from experience in software development, business modeling, management, and organizational learning and development. Her wide-ranging background allows her to root the concepts presented in *Creating Contagious Commitment* in today's real-world challenges.

Andrea designed and developed the Tipping Point computer simulation and workshop in 1997 after seeing so many well-meaning change efforts miss their mark. By demonstrating the dynamics that underpin effective change, the workshop gives managers new and innovative tools to maximize the success of their own change initiatives. She has delivered the workshop to corporations, professional organizations, and business schools across the United States. *Creating Contagious Commitment* grew out of a demand from workshop participants for more examples, theory, and background, all of which will appeal to any manager faced with implementing a significant organizational change.

After earning master's degrees in mathematics and psychology and a doctorate in behavioral decision making, Andrea went on to further studies at the Coaches Institute and the MIT Sloan Business School executive education program in system dynamics. She has served on the Graduate Faculty at UNC Chapel Hill and taught decision making at Pfeiffer University's graduate program in organizational management.

Printed in the United States
42056LVS00003BA/1-72

9 780974 102801